**New Directions for
Community Colleges**

Arthur M. Cohen
EDITOR-IN-CHIEF

Richard L. Wagoner
ASSOCIATE EDITOR

Gabriel Jones
MANAGING EDITOR

Student Athletes and Athletics

Linda Serra Hagedorn
David Horton, Jr.
EDITORS

Number 147 • Fall 2009
Jossey-Bass
San Francisco

STUDENT ATHLETES AND ATHLETICS
Linda Serra Hagedorn, David Horton, Jr. (eds.)
New Directions for Community Colleges, no. 147

Arthur M. Cohen, Editor-in-Chief
Richard L. Wagoner, Associate Editor
Gabriel Jones, Managing Editor

NEW DIRECTIONS FOR COMMUNITY COLLEGES (ISSN 0194-3081, electronic ISSN 1536-0733) is part of The Jossey-Bass Higher and Adult Education Series and is published quarterly by Wiley Subscription Services, Inc., A Wiley Company, at Jossey-Bass, 989 Market Street, San Francisco, California 94103-1741. Periodicals Postage Paid at San Francisco, California, and at additional mailing offices. POSTMASTER: Send address changes to New Directions for Community Colleges, Jossey-Bass, 989 Market Street, San Francisco, California 94103-1741.

SUBSCRIPTIONS cost $98.00 for individuals and $269.00 for institutions, agencies, and libraries in the United States. Prices subject to change.

EDITORIAL CORRESPONDENCE should be sent to the Editor-in-Chief, Arthur M. Cohen, at the Graduate School of Education and Information Studies, University of California, Box 951521, Los Angeles, California 90095-1521. All manuscripts receive anonymous reviews by external referees.

New Directions for Community Colleges is indexed in CIJE: Current Index to Journals in Education (ERIC), Contents Pages in Education (T&F), Current Abstracts (EBSCO), Ed/Net (Simpson Communications), Education Index/Abstracts (H. W. Wilson), Educational Research Abstracts Online (T&F), ERIC Database (Education Resources Information Center), and Resources in Education (ERIC).

Microfilm copies of issues and articles are available in 16mm and 35mm, as well as microfiche in 105mm, through University Microfilms Inc., 300 North Zeeb Road, Ann Arbor, Michigan 48106-1346.

CONTENTS

EDITORS' NOTES

In 2001, a volume of *New Directions for Student Services* titled Student Services for Athletes was edited by Mary F. Howard-Hamilton and Sherry K. Watt. Their volume covered a range of athletics-related issues with respect to four-year NCAA member institutions. The volume included important information on the evolution of college sports and the characteristics of student athletes, psychosocial and cognitive development of athletes, support services for female students and students of color, and the impact of national issues on college sports. Though extremely thorough, the volume spoke little about athletes or athletics at community colleges. In fact, generally speaking there is a large void in the literature concerning athletics at community colleges that is particularly problematic. This is the first volume of *New Directions for Community Colleges* that focuses on college athletics. This void is especially surprising and troubling when one considers that almost half (46 percent) of all undergraduates are enrolled in community colleges (American Association of Community Colleges, 2008). All student types are worthy of study. We are proud that community college athletes are finally acknowledged as an important student segment.

The current volume is a step toward correcting the dearth of literature specific to community college athletics by bringing scholars and practitioners from various academic disciplines and geographic locations together to share information, discussion, and research on issues related to athletics at the community college.

Purpose and Audience

A natural question may be, Why do we need athletics at community colleges? Community colleges serve as the gateway for students to enter and explore higher education. These institutions grant access to millions of students every year and are especially beneficial to those students who have limited or no access to four-year universities. Be it for reasons of family responsibility, financial concerns, or a history of academic difficulty, the fact remains that community colleges are often the *only* option for some students with dreams of postsecondary success (Hagedorn, in press). Community colleges are also the postsecondary choice for a large number of students of color who begin postsecondary training. The work of noted researchers has documented that community colleges' intercollegiate athletic programs serve as agents of entry to higher education (Doyle, 2006; Laanan, 2003). Together, community colleges and athletics annually foster postsecondary

access for thousands of high school graduates who wish to continue their education beyond high school.

It is a gross understatement to say that college athletics are a complex part of any institution's operation. Further, it may be that community college athletics present an even more multifaceted and murkier operational environment because of limited human and financial resources. Yet we know little about the unique scope of issues and challenges facing student athletes. Further, colleges and state data systems do not typically follow or analyze data pertaining to the transfer or other success of student athletes following their exit from the community college. Thus we know almost nothing of the effect of athletics on subsequent postsecondary or other ventures. As we examine issues related to community college athletics, it is not our intent to answer all pressing questions on these topics. Rather, our purpose is to offer a mechanism for further dialogue and improved practices, and to bring awareness of the importance of these issues for community colleges.

This volume of *New Directions for Community Colleges* is intended for a broad audience, including community college leaders, faculty, athletic staff and coaches, and researchers. The volume will interest not only those whose work focuses directly on student athletes and athletics but also everyone who values the community college and its role in promoting success among the many types of students. Chapters in this volume will also appeal to and benefit state-level policy makers and others who are genuinely concerned with the academic success of community college student athletes and the continued success of athletic programs as a whole.

Specifically, this volume focuses on the role of athletics at the community college and the impact on student athletes. The chapters explore various, interconnected topics pertaining to community college athletic programs and community college student athletes. As an underserved population, student athletes find their life and institutional experiences greatly different from those of other community college students as well as their four-year counterparts. This volume brings together a multitude of voices and perspectives from higher education professionals working with or researching athletics, specifically at community colleges. The volume also presents information on the best practices that have been instituted at community colleges across the United States.

Overview of Contents

We begin the volume with a highly informative chapter filled with facts, figures, and statistics from V. Barbara Bush and her colleagues. The chapter serves not only as a receptacle of information but also as a reference guide that will clearly underline the extent of community college athletic participation. We learn that more than five hundred community colleges actively participate in athletics and that these programs are used by a relatively large number of full-time students, a surprising 20 percent. Interestingly, smaller colleges and those in more rural areas are more apt to have an athletic program. This chapter serves as an excellent beginning to the volume and can be a useful reference for anyone interested in athletics at the community college level.

The second chapter, authored by David Horton, Jr., covers academic success and highlights a very important topic. Using a phenomenological paradigm, Horton argues for the benefits of athletic participation for community college students. However, he defines success using the voices of the students themselves. Rather than measure success in GPA, these students speak of maintaining eligibility and of being able to keep up with other students despite a grueling schedule that includes athletic training.

Shaun R. Harper's chapter on black male student athletes is sure to foment debate. Harper boldly incorporates critical race theory to advocate attention and supportive policies specific for male athletes at community colleges.

In whatever involvement the reader may have with respect to community college athletics, he or she will no doubt find the chapter written by Heather J. Lawrence and her colleagues to be useful and informative. This informational chapter has instructions in maintaining a quality community college athletic program and also guidance for those seeking to expand—or possibly even eliminate—such programs.

Chapters Five and Six, both written by Ellen J. Staurowsky, carry out an in-depth and extensive journey into gender equity as seen in community college athletic departments. Part One looks back and offers an overview of Title IX that includes deep description and the historical path and participation of the National Junior College Athletic Association (NJCAA). Part Two specifically delves into the present, with a bit of speculation for the future.

The penultimate chapter deals with the very important area of student services as related to athletics. Despite the fact that athletes often have a higher retention rate than their nonathlete counterparts, Jason Storch and Matthew Ohlson present information on how support structures may be better tailored for this significant group of students.

The last chapter poses a twist. Rather than extolling the virtue of community college athletics, this final chapter critically examines the practice and exposes the negatives. The chapter is designed to be a wake-up call for athletic programs and is presented to balance the coverage so that the critical reader will be presented with both sides.

We invite you to learn more about community college athletics and athletes. If you find an aspect missing from this discussion, please let us know so that we can include it as we begin our work on additional manuscripts regarding this highly important topic.

Linda Serra Hagedorn (lindah@iastate.edu)
David Horton, Jr. (hortond@ohio.edu)
Editors

NEW DIRECTIONS FOR COMMUNITY COLLEGES • DOI: 10.1002/cc

References

American Association of Community Colleges (AACC). "Research and Statistics." Retrieved Jan. 28, 2009, from http://www2.aacc.nche.edu/research/index.htm.

Doyle, W. R. "Community College Transfers and College Graduation." *Change,* 2006, *38*(3), 56–58.

Hagedorn, L. S. (in press). The pursuit of student success: The directions and challenges facing community colleges. In J. C. Smart (ed.), *Higher Education: Handbook of Theory and Research.* New York: Agathon Press.

Howard-Hamilton, M. F., and Watt, S. K. (eds). *Student Services for Athletes.* New Directions for Student Services, no. 93. San Francisco: Jossey-Bass, 2001.

Laanan, F. S. "Degree Aspirations of Two-Year College Students." *Community College Journal of Research and Practice,* 2003, 27, 495–518.

LINDA SERRA HAGEDORN is professor and director of the Research Institute for Studies in Education (RISE) at Iowa State University.

DAVID HORTON, JR., is an assistant professor in the department of counseling and higher education at Ohio University.

1

This chapter provides the numbers and statistics related to the five most popular men's and women's community college sports teams, athletically related scholarship aid, expenses, and other pertinent topics associated with athletics at the community college.

What the Numbers Say About Community Colleges and Athletics

V. Barbara Bush, Cindy Castañeda, David E. Hardy, Stephen G. Katsinas

Evidence clearly points to the presence of intercollegiate athletics at the early junior colleges established prior to World War I (Koos, 1925; Eells, 1931). Moving into more current times, we find among prominent reasons for institutional involvement with athletics giving students a "true college experience," expanding access (Castañeda, 2004), recruiting a more diverse student body (Bush, Castañeda, Katsinas, and Hardy, in press), and addressing the "missing male phenomenon" (Castañeda, Katsinas, and Hardy, 2008). This chapter uses national data to give an introductory overview regarding the depth and breadth of the involvement of America's community colleges in intercollegiate athletics. It presents more of a snapshot of what is currently occurring than an in-depth analysis of gender equity in intercollegiate athletics at community colleges. Chapters Five and Six of this volume offer more inclusive information specific to the history and impact of gender equity.

Methodology

This chapter draws on a national census of intercollegiate athletics at U.S. community colleges used as a part of a 2004 doctoral dissertation by Cindy Castañeda at the University of North Texas under the direction of Stephen G. Katsinas. Methodologically, the dissertation used U.S. Department of Education Integrated Postsecondary Education Data System or

IPEDS-assigned unique identification numbers (UNITID) to combine data from the 2002–03 and 2003–04 administrations of the Equity in Athletics Disclosure Act, IPEDS, and the 2005 Basic Classifications published by the Carnegie Foundation for the Advancement of Teaching (2006). The result was a comprehensive overview of athletics at public community colleges, excluding special-use institutions, tribal colleges, and two-year-under-four-year colleges.

Student Involvement in Community College Athletics

In the 2001–02 academic year, a total of 72,558 full-time students at 508 institutions participated in athletic teams fielded by U.S. community colleges, making intercollegiate athletics among the most popular activities found at American community colleges (Castañeda, 2004). With regard to gender, men outnumbered women participating across all college-sponsored sports: 26,698 students, or 37 percent, were women, while 45,860 or 63 percent were men.

There were major differences found in the level and extent of student involvement across specific types of community colleges. Among the 860 identifiable community college districts sending data to IPEDS, 508 (59 percent) chose to field athletic teams (Castañeda, Katsinas, and Hardy, 2006). However, colleges participating in intercollegiate athletics are not spread evenly across the three major geographic classifications under the new 2005 Basic Classifications of Associate's Colleges nomenclature released in February 2006 by the Carnegie Foundation for the Advancement of Teaching (Carnegie, 2006). Among the 508 institutions reporting involvement in intercollegiate athletics to IPEDS, 309, or 61 percent, are classified under Carnegie as rural, 129 (25 percent) as suburban, and 70, or 14 percent, as urban (Castañeda, Katsinas, and Hardy, 2006). Rural colleges accounted for 47 percent of all athletes at public community colleges, yet in 2002–03 they accounted for only 39 percent of full-time, degree-seeking students at community colleges. This disparity represents an important comparison baseline; only full-time degree-seeking students who meet academic requirements are eligible to participate in intercollegiate athletics. For this reason, analysis of the most popular sports and participants presented in the tables included in this chapter does not use unduplicated headcount; students participating in more than one sport will have multiple counts (Castañeda, Katsinas, and Hardy, 2006).

Table 1.1 presents data on full-time degree-seeking students participating in intercollegiate athletics at U.S. community colleges in the 2002–03 academic year by gender and by 2005 Carnegie Basic Classifications categories of Associate's Colleges. A total of 2,928,842 first-time degree-seeking students were enrolled in that year, of which 1,009,815, or 34 percent, were enrolled at rural community colleges, 903,806, or 31 percent, were enrolled at subur-

NEW DIRECTIONS FOR COMMUNITY COLLEGES • DOI: 10.1002/cc

Table 1.1. Full-Time Degree-Seeking Students Participating in Intercollegiate Athletics at Associate's Colleges in 2002–03, by Gender and by 2005 Carnegie Basic Classification

| | All First-Time Students Enrolled | | All Full-Time Student Athletes Enrolled | | | | | |
| | | | All | | Men | | Women | |
	Number	%	Number	%	Number	%	Number	%
Rural small	184,335	6	36,867	3	16,897	3	19,970	3
Rural medium	303,130	10	242,504	18	105,296	17	137,208	18
Rural large	522,350	18	261,175	19	121,418	20	139,757	19
Rural total	**1,009,815**	**34**	**540,546**	**39**	**243,611**	**40**	**296,935**	**40**
Suburban single	492,340	17	246,170	18	113,795	19	132,375	18
Suburban multi	411,466	14	205,733	15	94,800	15	110,933	15
Suburban total	**903,806**	**31**	**451,903**	**33**	**208,595**	**34**	**243,308**	**33**
Urban single	292,963	9	78,889	6	35,960	6	42,929	6
Urban multi	752,268	26	301,079	22	127,522	21	173,557	23
Urban total	**1,015,231**	**35**	**379,968**	**28**	**163,482**	**27**	**216,486**	**29**
Total	**2,928,842**	**100**	**1,372,417**	**100**	**615,688**	**100**	**756,729**	**100**

Note: Percentages may not add to 100 because of rounding. Data were compiled by Castañeda in 2006. It is important to note that these side-by-side comparisons were developed using two data years, owing to the timing of data released by the U.S. Department of Education and the derivation of the data from two surveys. Full-time degree-seeking comes from the IPEDS data. The data presented in Table 1.2 are unduplicated athlete headcount and come from the EADA data surveys.

ban community colleges, and 1,015,231, or 35 percent, were enrolled at urban community colleges. Comparing these data to all enrolled first-time student-athletes, we find 39 percent of all first-time student athletes enrolling at rural, 33 percent at suburban, and 28 percent at urban community colleges. As a percentage of all enrolled first-time students, the smaller the college the greater the likelihood of institutional participation in intercollegiate athletics, with student athletes making up 20 percent of all first-time students. This finding is consistent with Moeck (2005), who found serving student athletes to be a prime motivating factor for smaller community colleges to operate on-campus housing.

Table 1.1 indicates that student athletes constitute a higher percentage of all first-time community college students at rural and suburban community colleges than the percentage of all new enrolled first-time students. The table shows the importance of intercollegiate athletics in attracting new first-time students by gender, particularly for men. The third column under men and women in the table reveals that male student athletes are a larger percentage of all first-time students enrolled at every type of rural, suburban, and urban associate's college. Comparing the three types, one sees that intercollegiate athletics may be used as a tool to attract male first-time students at urban and suburban as well as rural community colleges. Male student athletes account for 6 percent of all first-time students enrolled at multi-campus urban and suburban community colleges, while first-time female student athletes are 2 percent and 3 percent respectively.

Table 1.2 presents data on participation in intercollegiate athletics, comparing those institutions that choose to award and those that choose not to award scholarship aid to student athletes, by Carnegie Associate's College Classification for 2002–03. Institutions that field intercollegiate athletic teams in the National Junior College Athletic Association's Divisions I and II award scholarship aid, while institutions fielding teams in Division III do not. Teams participating in the Northwest Athletic Association of Community Colleges award only partial scholarships and are thus roughly comparable to the NJCAA's Division II, while the 109 participating members of the Commission on Athletics at California's community colleges award no athletically related scholarship aid at all and for this reason are comparable to the NJCAA's Division III colleges. The first column of Table

Table 1.2. Community Colleges Participating in Intercollegiate Athletics, by Institutions Awarding and Not Awarding Scholarship Aid to Student Athletes and by 2005 Carnegie Basic Classification of Associate's College, 2002–03

| | Associate's Colleges with Athletics | Level of Athletic Competition | | | |
| | | Divisions I and II (with Scholarships) | | Division III (w/out Scholarships) | |
		Number	%	Number	%
Rural small	52	37	71	15	29
Rural medium	166	134	81	32	19
Rural large	90	68	76	22	24
Rural total	**308**	**239**	**78**	**69**	**22**
Suburban single	80	34	43	46	58
Suburban multi	67	29	43	38	57
Suburban total	**147**	**63**	**43**	**84**	**57**
Urban single	24	16	67	8	33
Urban multi	88	40	45	48	55
Urban total	**112**	**56**	**50**	**56**	**50**
Total	**567**	**358**	**63**	**209**	**7**

Note: Institutions in the NJCAA's Divisions I and II award scholarship aid, while institutions in Division III do not. Data were compiled by Castañeda in 2006. The data presented here come from the EADA data surveys.

1.2 lists each type of community college fielding athletic teams, while the next two columns, under the heading "Level of Athletic Competition," disaggregate that institutional data into Divisions I and II (with scholarships) and Division III (no scholarships). A majority of suburban community colleges do not offer athletically related aid, while the split is even for urban community colleges. In contrast, about four of every five rural community colleges offer athletically related aid, underscoring the importance that intercollegiate athletics may play as a recruitment tool.

Table 1.3 applies the new 2005 Carnegie Associate's College classifications to 2002–03 EADA data to show community colleges with intercollegiate athletics both in terms of the number of teams and average number of teams fielded by gender. It is important to note that, because some colleges may choose to field more men's teams than women's teams and vice versa, the total number of teams fielded in the first column ("All Community Colleges with Athletics") may not equal the total number of teams fielded by gender in the two columns that follow. Table 1.3 shows that the number of teams fielded is roughly equal across all college types, with a slightly higher average number of teams fielded for men than women at each type of college.

Table 1.3. Number of Teams by Gender and Average Number of Teams by Gender and by College Classification, 2002–03

	Associate's Colleges with Athletics	Total Number of Teams Fielded		Average Number of Teams Fielded	
		Men	Women	Men	Women
Rural small	52	58	48	3.1	2.8
Rural medium	166	166	168	3.2	3.1
Rural large	90	88	90	4.0	3.9
Rural total	**308**	**306**	**301**	**3.4**	**3.3**
Suburban single	80	80	78	5.0	4.7
Suburban multi	67	67	67	4.8	4.6
Suburban total	**147**	**147**	**145**	**4.9**	**4.6**
Urban single	24	24	24	4.0	3.7
Urban multi	88	88	88	4.3	4.2
Urban total	**112**	**112**	**112**	**4.2**	**4.1**
Total	**567**	**565**	**558**	**4.0**	**3.8**

Note: Some colleges may field more men's teams than women's teams, and vice versa, so the total number of teams fielded in the first column may not equal the breakdowns by gender in the next two columns. Data were analyzed by Castañeda (2006). It is important to note that these side-by-side comparisons were developed using two data years, because of the timing of data released by the U.S. Department of Education and the derivation of the data from two surveys. Full-time degree-seeking comes from the IPEDS data.

Table 1.4 presents men's and women's team sports at community colleges ranked by the number of athletic scholarships awarded and by expenses for 2002–03 according to Carnegie Associate's College type. When sports are ranked by the number of full and partial athletic scholarships awarded, basketball emerges with the largest number of students. A total of 317 scholarships are awarded to men and 295 to women. Baseball, with 294 scholarships awarded to men, and softball, with 263 scholarships to women, are the second most popular sports. For men, basketball and baseball are followed by golf (119 scholarships), soccer (101), and football (65). For women, basketball and softball are followed by volleyball (226), soccer (128), and tennis (71).

When the sports are ranked by expenses incurred at the institutions (as reported by the institutions to the federal government through the EADA Survey), football is far and away the most expensive sport to operate. Football, with an average expense of $99,705, average annual expense of $99,705 per team, is more than twice as expensive as the second- and

Table 1.4. Men's and Women's Team Sports Ranked by Scholarships Awarded and Expenses Incurred, 2002–03

	Ranked by Number of Full and Partial Scholarships Awarded		Ranked by Expenses Incurred by Colleges		
	Sport	Number	Sport	Number of Teams	Annual Expense per Team
Men's teams	Basketball	317	Football	129	$99,705
	Baseball	294	Baseball	438	$48,511
	Golf	119	Basketball	484	$43,354
	Soccer	101	Rodeo	37	$38,516
	Football	65	Ice hockey	7	$36,798
Women's teams	Basketball	295	Basketball	444	$39,703
	Softball	263	Softball	382	$34,388
	Volleyball	226	Volleyball	358	$25,810
	Soccer	28	Track and field, cross-country	34	$22,211
	Tennis	71	Rodeo	34	$19,689

Notes: Data were analyzed by Castañeda (2006) from the publications of the National Junior College Athletic Association and the Northwest Athletic Association of Community Colleges.

Institutions participating in NJCAA's Division I may award full scholarships including tuition, fees, room, board, and limited travel costs for student athletes, while NJCAA's Division II colleges can award partial scholarships not to exceed tuition and fees. NWAACC can award up to a maximum of $1,200 in work-study and are counted as awarding athletic aid. Athletically related expense data were compiled by Castañeda from the Equity in Athletics Disclosure Act (EADA) 2003 survey. Average expenses may not necessarily include in-kind contributions such as equipment and so on.

third-ranked men's sports, baseball ($48,511) and basketball ($43,354), and the most expensive women's sport, basketball ($39,703). As Table 1.4 indicates, the average reported expenses are much higher for men's sports than for women's, with the range for men between $99,705 for the most expensive sport (football) to $36,798 for the fifth most expensive (ice hockey). In contrast, the range of average expenses for women's sports at community colleges is far lower, from $39,703 for the most expensive sport (basketball) to just $19,689 for the fifth-ranked women's (sport rodeo).

Discussion

Intercollegiate athletics are clearly a popular student activity at community colleges. This is particularly true for rural community colleges. As Cohen and Brawer (2008) have noted, responsive community colleges tailor the range and scope of their academic and vocational curricula, offerings in developmental education, workforce training, and continuing education to needs in their service regions. The evidence is compelling that community-based strategies also guide sponsorship of intercollegiate athletics at community colleges.

Rural-serving colleges make the greatest commitment to intercollegiate athletics, as seen in student participation (see Table 1.1), relatively higher coaching salaries (Castañeda, 2004), larger awards of athletically related student aid (Castañeda, Katsinas, and Hardy, 2008), and the level of competition sponsored (see Table 1.2). One likely reason that rural community colleges emphasize athletics is the drive to maintain enrollment growth, which in turn benefits the college through increased efficiency and economies of scale in housing, food service, and student activities. It appears that the presence of athletics results in enrollment of more full-time students generally and more full-time male students in particular. These additional full-time students yield revenue in the form of increased state reimbursement to the college reimbursements that have been shown to bring in more income than the college expends on athletics (Castañeda, 2004). In an impact study of sports programs at California community colleges, Thein (2002) found that an athlete was valued at approximately $7,470 per academic year.

Intercollegiate athletics are a vital part of more than 58 percent of the 860 public community college districts across the United States (Castañeda, Katsinas, and Hardy, 2008). In 2002–03, 567 colleges sponsored competition in more than thirty sports, fielding 4,277 teams in which an unduplicated 72,558 student athletes participated (Castañeda, 2004). Ranked by the number of scholarships awarded, the top five men's sports in 2002–03 were basketball, baseball, golf, soccer, and football, and the top five women's sports were basketball, softball, volleyball, soccer, and tennis. By reported expenses, the top five men's sports were football, baseball, basketball, rodeo, and ice hockey, while the top five women's sports were basketball, softball, volleyball, track and field and cross-country, and rodeo. It should be noted that sports such as rodeo may receive a large volume of in-kind donations of equipment and support of animal maintenance that are not reported to the federal government. Large in-kind donations also may not be reported for football. We further note that these data do not incorporate well the large number of California's community colleges in football, which are prohibited from awarding full or partial athletic scholarships under Commission on Athletics guidelines.

Gender equity remains an important challenge in intercollegiate athletics at community colleges. The challenge is represented in Table 1.4, which shows that football is more than twice as expensive as the second-ranked men's sport or top-ranked women's sport. The presence of football challenges the institutions that sponsor it to achieve gender equity in aid to intercollegiate athletics, whether represented by proportional participation by sport or total number of participants. What is clear is that many more men than women participated across all college-sponsored sports (Bush, Castañeda, Katsinas, and Hardy, in press). By college type, participation is skewed heavily to the rural colleges, which accounted for 47 percent of all athletes at rural community colleges. In 2002–03, rural colleges accounted for only 39 percent of full-time degree-seeking students at community colleges. This percentage of full-time students provides an important baseline for comparison, because only full-time degree-seeking students who meet academic requirements can participate in intercollegiate athletics (Castañeda, 2004).

Implications

Because community colleges are active participants in intercollegiate athletics, they take on many of the issues facing four-year colleges and universities. This chapter has outlined access, gender equity, financial stability, and recruitment as four areas of concern. Later chapters in this volume by Ellen Staurowsky as well as Heather Lawrence and others will promote a more detailed discussion of these topics individually. Perhaps these concerns will raise questions in the future about the alignment of intercollegiate athletics with the mission of the community college. Do two-year institutions, in their focus on access, continue to view athletics as a way of recruiting students (especially males) who may not otherwise pursue higher education? If so, might institutions without intercollegiate athletics wish to consider adding them for recruitment purposes?

For those institutions considering the fielding of athletic teams, the issue of gender equity is somewhat more easily addressed by avoiding football altogether. We believe it is possible that some institutions already participating in intercollegiate athletics in the NJCAA's Division III, which does not award athletically related scholarship aid, may choose to shift to Divisions I or II, which do, in order to accomplish the purposes outlined here. Those institutions adding athletically related aid should consider participation in baseball or softball and basketball, for both cost and gender equity reasons. Because the nation is in recession, finances will surely dictate certain choices, and we would not recommend that intercollegiate athletics be initiated at the expense of academic endeavors. Still, we recognize that as an engagement tool, community colleges generally and urban community colleges specifically may consider following the lead of rural and suburban community colleges engaged in intercollegiate athletics and initiate additional programs. In particular, those colleges that are considering initiating or adding sports should appraise sports that are popular in their feeder high schools, including but not limited to basketball, baseball and softball, women's volleyball, and soccer.

References

Bush, V. B., Castañeda, C., Hardy, D. E., and Katsinas, S. G. "Athletics in Community Colleges: A Primer." In M. T. Miller and D. B. Kissinger (eds.), *Community College Student Athletes*. Charlotte, N.C.: Greenwood/Information Age, in press

Carnegie Foundation for the Advancement of Teaching. 2006. *2005 Basic Classification of Institutions of Higher Education*. http://www.carnegiefoundation.org/classifications/index.asp?key=791 (accessed Aug. 31, 2008).

Castañeda, C. "A National Overview of Intercollegiate Athletics in Public Community Colleges." (Doctoral dissertation, University of North Texas). *Dissertation Abstracts International*, 2004, *65*/08, 2915A.

Castañeda, C., Katsinas, S. G., and Hardy, D. E. "The Importance of Intercollegiate Athletics at Rural-Serving Community Colleges: A Policy Brief by the Education Policy Center at the University of Alabama for the MidSouth Partnership for Rural Community Colleges." 2006. http://www.ruralcommunitycolleges.org/docs/MSPBRIEFATHLETICS.pdf (accessed Aug. 14, 2008).

Castañeda, C., Katsinas, S. G., and Hardy, D. E. *Meeting the Challenge of Gender Equity in Community College Athletics*. New Directions for Community Colleges, no. 142. San Francisco: Jossey-Bass, 2008.

Cohen, A. M., and Brawer, F. B. *The American Community College* (5th ed.). San Francisco: Jossey-Bass, 2008.

Eells, W. C. *The Junior College*. Boston: Houghton Mifflin, 1931.

Koos, L. V. *The Junior College Movement*. Minneapolis: University of Minnesota Press, 1925.

Moeck, P. G. "An Analysis of On-Campus Housing at Public Rural Community Colleges in the United States." (Doctoral dissertation, University of North Texas). *Dissertation Abstracts International*, 2005, *66*/06, 2079.

National Junior College Athletic Association. *NJCAA Handbook and Casebook 2002–2003*. Denver: NJCAA, 2002.

Northwest Athletic Association of Community Colleges. "Member Schools." 2004a. http://www.nwaacc.org/memberSchools.php (accessed Feb. 7, 2004).

Northwest Athletic Association of Community Colleges. "NWAACC History." 2004b. http://www.nwacc.org/history/htm (accessed Jan. 27, 2004).

Thein, P. J. "Feather River College Original Feasibility Study for Additional Sports Programs with Follow-up Data." Paper presented at the meeting of the American Association of Community Colleges, Apr. 3–6, 2002, in Minneapolis, Minnesota.

U.S. Department of Education. *Equity in Athletic Disclosure Act Survey 2003–2004*. [Data file]. Washington, DC: U.S. Department of Education, 2003.

U.S. Department of Education. "The Athletic Disclosure Web Site." 2004. http://surveys.ope.ed.gov/athletics/ (accessed Feb. 29, 2004).

V. BARBARA BUSH *is an associate professor in the Department of Counseling and Higher Education at the University of North Texas.*

CINDY CASTAÑEDA *currently serves as the executive dean of the School of Ethnic Studies, Social Studies, and Physical Education at Richland College (Texas).*

DAVID E. HARDY *is an assistant professor of higher education and director of research of the Education Policy Center at the University of Alabama.*

STEVE G. KATSINAS *has served since 2005 as professor of higher education administration and the director of the Education Policy Center at the University of Alabama.*

2

This chapter examines the impact of athletic participation on community college students through reflective commentaries provided by current and former community college student athletes.

Class and Cleats: Community College Student Athletes and Academic Success

David Horton, Jr.

At four-year colleges and universities sports are generally categorized as either revenue- or nonrevenue-generating (Upthegrove, Roscigno, and Charles, 1999). A revenue-generating sport is one that provides an institution with financial resources (or income) beyond what is necessary to financially sustain the specific team or the institution's athletic program. The term *revenue-generating* is most often associated with sports such as men's baseball, football, and basketball as well as women's basketball, softball, and volleyball (Sawyer, 1993; Upthegrove, Roscigno, and Charles, 1999). However, it is unusual to hear these terms used in conjunction with junior or community college athletic teams or programs, which rarely produce revenues substantial enough to be termed self-sustaining.

According to the Equity in Athletics Disclosure Act (EADA) 2006 survey, approximately 49 percent (212) of the 430 National Junior College Athletic Association (NJCAA) member institutions reported either a financial loss or no positive financial gain (total revenues net total athletic expenses) in 2006. Of the remaining 218 institutions surveyed, 23 percent (101) earned revenues at or above $25,000, while only 4 percent (18) earned revenues at or above $150,000. These totals for NJCAA member institutions pale in comparison to their four-year institutional counterparts. For example, according to the 2006 EADA survey, the University of Texas at Austin

New Directions for Community Colleges, no. 147, Fall 2009 © 2009 Wiley Periodicals, Inc.
Published online in Wiley InterScience (www.interscience.wiley.com) • DOI: 10.1002/cc.374

15

and the University of Michigan at Ann Arbor reported net revenues from athletic programs of $15-20 million during the 2006 year.

In light of these findings, it is worth asking what the value is of community college athletic programs if they do not generate substantial revenues for the sponsoring institution. Or, phrased differently, if athletic programs are a financial drain on institutional resources, why do institutions continue to support them? This is a significant question because the reaction will certainly vary with the position of the responder. For instance, a current or former community college student athlete may respond with a reminder that not everything that counts can (or should) be counted in dollars and cents. A coach or athletic administrator will extol the values of athletics that complement the training entrusted to colleges.

From a community college context, the financial return of an institution's investment in an athletic program and investment in students by providing opportunities for athletic participation is indeed impossible to measure. Compared to many large athletic programs at four-year institutions, athletic programs at the community college do not share the luxury of a fixation on packed stadiums, product endorsements, or million-dollar television contracts (Upthegrove, Roscigno, and Charles, 1999). For many community colleges, "what counts" is creating opportunities for access to higher education for students, especially those from underprivileged socioeconomic or underrepresented racial and ethnic backgrounds; fostering co-curricular activities for students; and giving students a chance to make a new start academically (Boulard, 2008; Castañeda, Katsinas, and Hardy, 2006; London, 2001; Peltier, Laden, and Matranga, 1999). Moreover, athletic programs are a parallel extension of community colleges' open access mission, enhancing individual academic and athletic skills, building social and human capital through sport participation, and developing personal discipline through academic study and athletic participation (Castañeda, Katsinas, and Hardy, 2006; Duderstadt, 2002; Laanan, Hardy, and Katsinas, 2006). Although these opportunities are real and important, they cannot be easily counted or quantified.

Research Objectives and Motivation

Knowledge of the value or benefit of athletic programs and student participation at the community college is a topic that has yet to be fully explored. Issues pertaining to community college athletes and athletics have received far less attention in both research-based and practitioner-based literatures (Umbach, Palmer, Kuh, and Hannah, 2006), compared to their four-year counterparts. Furthermore, much of the literature that is available on this topic is presented in a deficit model: student athletes don't graduate, big-time athletic programs are bad for institutions, athletic programs' obsession with state-of-the-art stadiums and bigger programs conflicts with development of improved academic buildings and programs (for example, Shulman and Bowen, 2001; Bowen and Levin, 2003; Sperber, 2000). Minimal attention has been given to sports' positive achievements, especially the academic and personal impact on athletes at the community college (Mangold, Bean, and Adams, 2003).

In an attempt to extend the current literature and close the chasm currently observed in the literature on this topic, this chapter explores the impact of athletic participation on community college students' academic planning and success. This chapter gives voice to student athletes and their perspectives and interpretations of their unique collegiate experience. Toward this end, the primary question that served as the guide for the present exploration is, What role do institutions and athletic participation play in producing successful students at the community college?

I begin this exploration with a brief review of the literature on this topic, discuss the sample and methods used in the analysis of data, and then present major patterns and themes found in the shared experiences of current and former community college athletes. Lastly, I reflect on and make suggestions for practitioners and administrators at the community college to consider.

Background

For many years, athletes and athletics have been synonymous with academic underachievement. Athletes have long been perceived to be less prepared, less motivated, and less intelligent than the general student population (Hobneck, Mudge, and Turchi, 2003; Mangold, Bean, and Adams, 2003). For example, studies such as those conducted by Knapp and Raney (1988) and Sawyer (1993) have brought to the forefront questionable patterns in community college athletes' course enrollment behaviors. These studies have suggested that athletes enroll in "easy" curricula to increase GPA for the sole purpose of remaining eligible for athletic participation. Knapp and Raney (1988) and Sawyer (1993) found that physical education departments are often the leading source of credit for student athletes and that grades earned in these courses are, on average, higher than those earned in other nonphysical education credit courses.

In addition to concerns about student athletes' in-class performance and course selection, many critics have raised concerns that college sports interfere with students' academic pursuits. Athletic participation has long been viewed by faculty members and critics as a hindrance to students' success in the classroom and associated with a decreased graduation rate (Bowen and Levin, 2005; Duderstadt, 2002; Shulman and Bowen, 2001). The perception is that student athletes are overly concerned and occupied with activities associated with sport, such that they devote minimal attention and focus to their academic studies and development (Simons, Bosworth, Fujita, and Jensen, 2007).

These arguments and others have severely weakened the belief that student athletes are truly students before athletes. Although this chapter acknowledges that students and athletes are motivated by various factors throughout their academic tenure, it aims to highlight some of the positive

NEW DIRECTIONS FOR COMMUNITY COLLEGES • DOI: 10.1002/cc

effects of athletic participation and sports as well as institutional and individual factors on student's success.

This chapter explores the experiences of student athletes through reflective commentaries within a phenomenological framework. A phenomenological framework emphasizes how individuals perceive their physical and social environment and the meaning they apply to their individual experiences (Crotty, 2003; Saha, 1978). Examining the experiences of athletes within a phenomenological paradigm affords a glimpse of the community college experience through the meaning-making process of the athlete. Through analysis of individual interview transcript data, I offer a discussion of the impact and benefit of athletic participation for students and provide examples of how these benefits extend beyond athletics.

Community College Access and Athletics

For more than a century, American community colleges have held a universal commitment to establishing an entryway to higher education for all students who desire admission (Hagedorn, in press). Accordingly, three general statements can be made about community colleges: (1) they serve as a viable entryway for students to enter and explore higher education; (2) their open door policy, low cost, flexible class scheduling, and close proximity to the "community" they serve increase the participation rate for many underserved and nontraditional students; and (3) they foster further opportunities through sponsorship of athletics for student involvement, community enhancement, and an enriched collegiate experience (Boulard, 2008; Castañeda, Katsinas, and Hardy, 2006; Hagedorn, in press; London, 1992; and Peltier, Laden, and Matranga, 1999).

Substantial increases in student enrollment in recent years have illustrated the expanding role community colleges play in affording access to postsecondary education for students of all backgrounds and academic proficiency. Additionally, access to higher education via the community college is further augmented and influenced through sponsorship of athletic programs. Growth in student enrollment through athletics is rarely attributed to the "Flutie Factor" phenomenon (Mixon, Trevino, and Minto, 2004), but instead to institutions' commitment to athletic recruitment. Nonetheless, increased enrollment at community colleges is realized through recruitment of prospective students for the purpose of full-time enrollment and athletic participation.

It is desirable for growth in student enrollment via athletics to result in a larger number of students completing academic requirements that lead to degree or certificate attainment (interview with "Bill Elliot," pseudonym, Mar. 28, 2008). This desire for heightened degree outcomes is especially true for institutions in the forty-two states where state funding for higher education is tied either directly or loosely to the performance of individual campuses or individual student success indicators (McLendon, Hearn, and Deaton, 2006).

NEW DIRECTIONS FOR COMMUNITY COLLEGES • DOI: 10.1002/cc

Academic Success

In the current climate of declining financial resources for institutions and greater interest in student outcomes, collection and dissemination of student outcomes data has become paramount (Dougherty and Kienzl, 2006). As a result, a trend has emerged toward research focused on the retention and academic success of such diverse subgroups as adult learners, e-learners, and nontraditional and racial and ethnic student groups. Investigating retention trends of student subgroups is a great asset to better understand the impending global problem of student retention and persistence. The study of athletes' institutional and system success is also of benefit to administrators who debate the influence and impact of athletics on students' academic gains. Continued study of athletes ultimately equips practitioners with empirical data to better assist them in their daily role as support systems for students and athletes.

As the first step for many students to the baccalaureate degree, the community college must ensure that the mission and purpose of academic pursuit remains a reality (Hagedorn, in press). It is important to note, however, that success can be applied to varying degrees of accomplishment experienced by students during their academic tenure. Throughout the higher education literature various student accomplishments have been employed to measure student success, among them GPA, job placement, transfer to a four-year institution, and professional certificate and associate degree attainment. For that reason, Floyd (1988) suggests "academic success" is a "value-laden" term used to signify completion of a student's intended educational goals or aspirations. Braxton (2003) asserts that both institutions and individuals define success as it relates to the extent to which each achieves intended goals.

For student athletes at the community college, "success" takes on a somewhat different connotation and meaning. In this chapter, student athletes are somewhat distinctive examples of what it means to be successful, how they gauge and measure their own success, and the factors that most contribute to their success as students and athletes. Students in this study defined success as finding personal happiness, passing all of their classes, maintaining athletic eligibility each semester, and having a good athletic season both individually and collectively. Gary, a former community college student athlete now attending a four-year institution, remarked that "passing every class and being eligible to play baseball is definitely . . . I consider that a success, maybe a small one but definitely a success." Another student, Patrick, described his own success as not only coming to realize the importance of his academic performance but also being able to fulfill his life goal to attend and participate in athletics at a Division I institution.

For these students, success is described as meeting academic requirements necessary to continue athletic participation at the community college and being productive enough in the classroom and in their sport to continue in athletics at a four-year institution following their years at the community college.

NEW DIRECTIONS FOR COMMUNITY COLLEGES • DOI: 10.1002/cc

Sample and Methods

Data for this study were collected through one-on-one interviews with current and former community college athletes. Current community college students and institutions were selected using the 2007 preseason and postseason football rankings and the 2008 men's preseason baseball rankings as released by the NJCAA. These particular rankings were selected to capture a national sample of students and represented institutions. Combined, a total of twenty-eight institutions and sixteen states were represented in all three rankings. Institutions noted in the "top fifteen" of each poll were contacted and requested to participate. Athletic directors (ADs) or coaches at each institution were sent letters electronically and via U.S. mail describing the nature of the study; they were requested to select students from their institutions to participate. Institutional contacts were also sent student information surveys and informed consent forms to distribute to student athletes along with return envelopes with prepaid postage.

To gain the student voices of community college athletes after their transfer to four-year institutions, three four-year universities and colleges were selected using convenience sampling methods (Creswell, 2002). From my access to institutions located in the southwest, northwest, and southeast regions of the United States, I selected a large Research I institution, a regional institution, and a private liberal arts institution.

Within eight weeks of initial contact with institutions, seventeen students returned student information forms and agreed to participate in a follow-up phone interview. The total student sample included eight female and nine male students, six students of color (African American and Hispanic), and eleven white non-Hispanic students; there were representatives from six men's and women's sport teams (baseball, basketball, football, soccer, softball, and volleyball). Eight students were enrolled at the community college at the time of the study; the remaining students were attending a four-year institution. According to self-reported data provided by the participants, the average community college GPA was 3.08, ACT score 21, and SAT score just above 1070.

Because of unavoidable academic and athletic obligations of the initial group of seventeen students, only eight of the seventeen who completed and returned a student information and consent form participated in a single semistructured phone interview, ranging from twenty to forty minutes in length. Within this group were three students located at the community college and five attending a four-year institution. All three of the community college students were nonscholarship athletes; all of the four-year students who were interviewed received either partial or full athletic scholarship while enrolled at the community college.

The interview participants were split equally between males and females but were unevenly distributed by race, with seven white students and one student of color. All interviews were conducted by phone, audio recorded, and later transcribed. Interview transcripts were then analyzed for common themes.

Data Analysis

Major and subcodes were created on the basis of like-minded pieces of data from each transcript. Definitions and explanations of codes through formulation of semantic relationships were created to facilitate organization of data. Once all spreadsheets with semantic relationships and codes were created and data from transcripts were categorized, major codes and subcodes were condensed where needed. From within these final categories, several themes emerged, with three most salient to the experiences of athletes and most helpful in permitting further insight into the shared experiences of this student group. Specifically, themes regarding the community college difference, academic commitment, and shared responsibility became evident as students discussed their personal experiences at the community college, academic success, and what it means to be a successful student and student athlete. Further discussions of each of these themes, along with examples from the data, are in the following section.

Findings

Before delving into student experiences at the community college, it is important to discuss students' process for selecting the community college as their institution of choice. Though several students in this study were academically eligible to attend a four-year institution on completion of their high school diploma, their reasons for attending a community college included the ability to stay at home while attending college, less expensive tuition, a higher level of comfort with a smaller institution, reservations about personal preparedness to be successful at a large college or university, and the opportunity to continue their dream by participating in athletics. Alisa, a student softball player attending a community college, stated that, being from a small town, she was more attracted to her community college because it was small and located in a small town. She explained that "it felt like something I was used to, so it made the transition [to college] much easier." Isabel, a first-year community college student, had this to say:

> I wasn't really ready for a big university yet and I came from small, you know, Catholic school so I wanted to go to a smaller school, and [this college] is small. . . . I know where all my classes are and I usually see some of the people I went to high school with.

Laura, another community college student in her second year, discussed the low cost and the opportunity to play softball in college, even though she was not given an athletic scholarship, as a primary factor in deciding to attend a community college: "It [my decision to attend a community college] was mostly a money issue, and I decided that it be [sic] better off to stay at home a couple of more years." In looking at factors specifically related to athletics, Andy, a four-year transfer student, attributed the opportunity to play baseball as the sole motivation for considering a community college. When asked about the impact of athletics in his school choice, he responded: "I really wanted to play baseball. That's what I love to do my whole life and I really didn't have any other options, so I really didn't consider anything else."

The Community College Difference. Regardless of the reasons given by students for attending a community college, students perceived their time spent at their respective institutions to be a valuable learning experience and a foundation for their personal growth. As students discussed their experiences, they vividly described how their time spent at the community college benefited them as students and as athletes. Major benefits included the ease with which students connected with faculty and the willingness of faculty to build relationships with students.

Researchers have long discussed the benefit of meaningful interactions between students and faculty members as an essential element of a quality learning experience (Kuh, Jillian, Schuh, Whit, and associates, 2005). Opportunities for such student-faculty relationships are increased in a learning environment with small class size, such as that provided at the community college. For students, the class size difference, compared to the four-year institutions students in the sample later attended, truly made the difference. Andy, a student at a regional four-year institution, described his academic experience this way: "The teachers really cared about you and that was a big thing for me . . . they were more than willing to help you out." Another student remarked that teachers "were really committed to the students there, making sure they are successful and I really felt like I could go to anyone there for any kind of help." Another student discussed the advantage of small classes as an opportunity for faculty members to know him personally. "I was really able to get to know my teachers and they were able to get to know me."

Academic Commitment. In a 1985 study, Adler and Adler reported that student athletes often develop strong athletic identities, the defining characteristic of which is the tendency to commit exclusively to a single athletic role at the expense of meaningful exploration of other available roles. However, for students in this study commitment to sport did not supersede their commitment to their academic studies; students' commitment to their sport, team, and coaches increased their desire to stay eligible and maintain their academic studies.

Students in this study also discussed the impact of participation in athletics on their personal discipline, academic studies, and creation of long-lasting social and support networks. Alisa described how participation in athletics made her a more disciplined student and a more disciplined athlete: "I think that athletics make you more disciplined and I think that part of it carried over to academics." Over the course of another interview, Clarke described his experiences as a student at a small rural institution, noting how its rural isolation from major distractions allowed him to better focus on both athletics and his academic studies. He commented, "Where I was at, there wasn't a whole lot to do except go to school and play baseball, so it allowed me to focus just on those two things, and it's helped me develop a work ethic for not only for athletics but for my academics." Another student, Isabel, stated, "I think [athletics] motivates me to do well in school; [if] I don't make the grades in school then obviously I can't play on the field, so I think it kind of balances itself out—I wanted to play so I have to do good in school."

Institutions' Commitment to Student Athletes. Many institutions find themselves in an undesirable situation when a focus on winning and developing successful athletic programs overshadows the focus and purpose of the fundamental establishment of sport (Duderstadt, 2002; Reapple, Peery, and Hohman, 1982). Athletics, as an extension of the institutional mission, constitutes a mechanism in which institutions can further support the personal and athletic goals of their student-athlete population. This balanced approach of supporting both students and athletic programs is manifested through institutions' evenly balanced financial commitment and implementation of policies geared toward athletic program growth and the academic success of those who participate.

One student described the commitment of his institution during his interview: "[The college] was very supportive . . . they encouraged you to do well in your school work and they encouraged people to come out and watch you, it was a very supportive student body." In addition to these expressions of support, the availability of student services such as those discussed by Storch and Ohlson in a later chapter of this volume are also examples of institutional commitment to student athletes and athletics. Courtney discussed the impact that participation in a student-led athletic council had on her own success as a student and athlete. According to Courtney, a council made up of selected representatives from each athletic team meets regularly to "talk about certain issues that pertain to sports and academics like steroid use and the amount of sleep that you should get at night." As team representatives on the athletic council, students bring back pamphlets and information about the topics discussed that week to share with their teammates during scheduled team meetings. Resources and outlets for students such as these described by Courtney enforce the idea that student athletes are supported by their institution and coaches.

Considerations and Ponderings

Many times on college campuses, athletics and other extracurricular activities are viewed as auxiliaries to activities taking place in the classroom. In reality, athletics and academics are intricately linked beyond the superficial requirement that students must be enrolled full-time to compete on athletic teams. As presented in this study, students spoke at length about the impact of support and encouragement provided by coaches, the institution, and institutional representatives. This was by and large the most important aspect discussed by students during interviews. Regardless of the reasons they stated for attending a community college, the "friendly" and "encouraging" environment of the community college was a major reason they excelled as both students and athletes.

Over the years, many community college presidents, administrators, and faculty members have expressed the idea that athletics at community colleges is not about the spectator but rather the development and growth of the student athlete. To be truly student-focused, athletics needs to be a vital part of the institution, not considered as a secondary add-on. Reapple, Peery, and Hohman wrote in 1982 that "unless athletics sponsored by the college are truly a part of the college education process and support and promote the goals of the institution, then the entire mission of the institution is in jeopardy and the athletic program has no basis for existence" (p. 162).

Roueche and Baker, in their 1987 book *Access and Excellence: Dream or Reality,* state that community colleges are a success when they are less focused on the skills students bring to college and more focused and intentional in developing the skills students have when they leave. For students represented in this study, their collegiate experiences and subsequent success as student and athlete was enhanced through the support and encouragement of both participation in athletics and attending a community college. Understanding the academic, personal, and athletic goals of student athletes is the first step to ensuring that students leave the institution more highly evolved and prepared than when they entered.

Conclusion and Implications

So what do we take from the experiences of these current and former community college student athletes? The responsibility for and sole dedication to student athletes' success does not begin and end with the athletic coaches or the athletic office. It has often been said that it takes a village to raise a child, but it may also be true that it takes more than a coach to make a successful student athlete. It is imperative that coaches and institutional leaders agree on the role of each in developing successful student athletes, what it means to have successful athletic programs, and their role in making sure both student and program success are achieved.

Many times coaches have limited influence on campus but find creative ways to influence student athletes to perform on the field or court. In the same vein, very few college presidents or faculty members can organize a fourth-quarter comeback or a ninth-inning rally, but they have the political savvy to explain to the academic community the importance of athletics and student athletes to their institution. The two parts must be integrated in order to successfully merge class and cleats. This synergy is accomplished through:

- Investment in athletic and academic support staff to ensure student athletes are on track to accomplish their goals, whether degree attainment, transfer, or professional development
- Provision of available funds for resources for both students and student athletes, which include but are not limited to counseling (academic and personal), tutoring, and personal growth and development workshops
- Encouragement of faculty to be actively involved in the athletic program and in the lives of student athletes as tutors, advocates, and faculty representatives to the athletic department

In the earlier pages of this chapter the question was posed: If community college athletic programs do not generate substantial revenues for the sponsoring institution, what is their value or worth to the institution? From the findings in this study and the commentaries provided by students, we can say that athletic programs at the community college offer a valuable experience for student participants and facilitate the continued desire to pursue academic endeavors beyond sports. It is agreed that it is becoming more expensive for institutions to fund programs at postsecondary institutions, especially athletic programs, in the turbulent economic times we currently face. To students in this study, and many others who are represented through the voices of the few, athletic programs at the community college are an extension of learning opportunities that cannot be measured by dollars and cents.

References

Adler, P., and Adler, P. A. "From Idealism to Pragmatic Detachment: The Academic Performance of College Athletics." *Sociology of Education,* 1985, *58,* 241–250.

Boulard, G. "Athletics Can Provide a Shot in the Arm." *Community College Times,* Aug. 1, 2008. Retrieved Aug. 26, 2008, from http://www.communitycollegetimes.com/Article.cfm?ArticleId=1095.

Bowen, W. G., and Levin, S. A. *Reclaiming the Game: College Sports and Educational Values.* Princeton, N.J.: Princeton University Press, 2005.

Braxton, J. M. "Student Success." In S. R. Komives, Jr., and D. B. Woodard and Associates (eds.), *Student Services: A Handbook for the Profession.* San Francisco: Jossey-Bass, 2003.

Castañeda, C., Katsinas, S. G., and Hardy, D. E. *The Importance of Intercollegiate Athletics at Rural-Serving Community Colleges. A Policy Brief by the Education Policy Center at the University of Alabama for the MidSouth Partnership for Rural Community Colleges,* 2006. Retrieved Aug. 14, 2008, from http://www.ruralcommunitycolleges.org/docs/MSPBRIEFATHLETICS.pdf .

Creswell, J. W. *Educational Research: Planning, Conducting, and Evaluating Quantitative and Qualitative Research.* Columbus, Ohio: Merrill Prentice Hall, 2002.

Crotty, M. *The Foundations of Social Research: Meaning and Perspective in the Research Process.* London: Sage, 2003.

Dougherty, K. J., and Kienzl, G. S. "It's Not Enough to Get Through the Open Door: Inequalities by Social Background in Transfer from Community Colleges." *Teachers College Record,* 2006, *108,* 452–487.

Duderstadt, J. J. *Intercollegiate Athletics and the American University.* Ann Arbor: University of Michigan Press, 2002.

Floyd, D. L. *Toward Mastery Leadership: Strategies for Student Success. Summary Report of a Colloquium.* Columbia, Md.: American College Testing Program, 1988.

Hagedorn, L. S. "The Pursuit of Student Success: Community College Interventions, Supports and Programs." In J. C. Smart (ed.), *Higher Education: Handbook of Theory and Research.* New York: Agathon, in press.

Hobneck, C., Mudge, L., and Turchi, M. *Improving Student Athlete Academic Success and Retention.* Chicago: Saint Xavier University and SkyLight Professional Development Field-Based Master's Program, 2003.

Knapp, T. J., and Raney, J. F. "Student-Athletes at Two-Year Colleges: Transcript Analysis of Grades and Credits." *Community Junior College Quarterly of Research and Practice,* 1988, *12,* 99–105.

Kuh, G. D., Kinzie, J., Schuh, J. H., Whitt, E. J., and associates. *Student Success in College: Creating Conditions That Matter.* San Francisco, 2005.

Laanan, F. S., Hardy, D. E., and Katsinas, S. G. "Documenting and Assessing the Role of Community Colleges in Developing Human Capital." *Community College Journal of Research and Practice,* 2006, 30, 855–869.

London, H. "College Athletes Who Never Graduate." *Academic Questions,* 1992, 6(1), 10–11.

Mangold, W. D., Bean, L., and Adams, D. "The Impact of Intercollegiate Athletics on Graduation Rates Among NCAA Division I Universities: Implications for College Persistence Theory and Practice." *Journal of Higher Education,* 2003, 74(5), 540–562.

McLendon, M. K., Hearn, J. C., and Deaton, R. "Called to Account: Analyzing the Origins and Spread of State Performance-Accountability Policies for Higher Education." *Educational Evaluation and Policy Analysis,* 2006, 28(1), 1–24.

Mixon, F. G., Jr., Trevino, L. J., and Minto, T. C. "Touchdowns and Test Scores: Exploring the Relationship Between Athletics and Academics." *Applied Economics Letters,* 2004, *11*(7), 421–424.

Peltier, G., Laden, R., and Matranga, M. "Student Persistence in College: A Review of Research." *Journal of College Student Retention,* 1999, *1*(4), 357–375.

Reapple, R., Peery, D. and Hohman, H. "Athletics in Community and Junior Colleges." In J. Frey (ed.), *The Governance of Intercollegiate Athletics.* West Point: Leisure Press, 1982.

Roueche, J. E., and Baker, G. A., III. *Access and Excellence: The Open Door College.* Washington, D.C.: Community College Press, 1987.

Saha, L. J. "The 'New' Sociology of Education and the Study of Learning Environments: Prospects and Problems." *Acta Sociologica,* 1978, *21*(1), 47–63.

Sawyer, D. T. *Analysis of Sport Participation on Retention of Community College Transfer Students at a California State University.* (1993). Retrieved from ProQuest Digital Dissertations. (AAT 9323947)

Shulman, J., and Bowen, W. *The Game of Life: College Sports and Educational Values.* Princeton, N.J.: Princeton University Press, 2001.

Simons, H. D., Bosworth, C., Fujita, S., and Jensen, M. "The Athlete Stigma in Higher Education." *College Student Journal,* 2007, *41*(2), 251–273.

Sperber, M., *Beer and Circus: How Big-Time College Sports Is Crippling Undergraduate Education.* New York: Holt, 2000.

Umbach, P. D., Palmer, M. M., Kuh, G. D., and Hannah, S. J. "Intercollegiate Athletes and Effective Educational Practices: Winning Combination or Losing Effort?" *Research in Higher Education,* 2006, 47(6), 709–733.

Upthegrove, T. R., Roscigno, V. J., and Charles, C. Z. "Big Money Collegiate Sports: Racial Concentration, Contradictory Pressures, and Academic Performance." *Social Science Quarterly*, 1999, *80*(4), 718–737.

U.S. Department of Education. *Equity in Athletic Disclosure Act Survey 2006–2007*. [Data file]. Washington, D.C.: U.S. Department of Education, 2006.

DAVID HORTON, JR., is a former Panola College and Dallas Baptist University student athlete and is currently an assistant professor in the Department of Counseling and Higher Education at Ohio University.

3

Critical Race Theory is used to consider the educational outcomes that could accrue when the interests of black male student athletes converge productively with the interests of community college administrators, faculty, and coaches.

Race, Interest Convergence, and Transfer Outcomes for Black Male Student Athletes

Shaun R. Harper

As indicated throughout this volume, much has been published about the experiences of student athletes in higher education. Some researchers have offered important insights into the psychosocial and identity-related challenges these students commonly face (Martin, 2009; Parham, 1993; Pinkerton, Hinz, and Barrow, 1989; Sedlacek and Adams-Gaston, 1992), while others have written about various issues related to career planning, academic motivation, and postcollege outcomes (Adler and Adler, 1987; Gaston-Gayles, 2004; Miller and Kerr, 2002; Pascarella and Smart, 1991; Pascarella and others, 1999; Simons, Van Rheenen, and Covington, 1999). A smaller body of literature has focused specifically on black male participation in college sports (Beamon, 2008; Benson, 2000; Donnor, 2005; Martin and Harris, 2006; Messer, 2006; Person and LeNoir, 1997). This research has been almost exclusively concerned with student athletes at four-year colleges and universities, and mostly at the National Collegiate Athletic Association's (NCAA) Division I competition level. Consequently, much remains to be known about community college student athletes in general and black male sports participants at those institutions specifically.

The aforementioned studies on black male student athletes at four-year institutions mostly describe racial differences in educational outcomes between them and their white male teammates. In his analyses of graduation rate data from the NCAA, Harper (2006) found that across four cohorts

of college student athletes 47 percent of black men graduated within six years, compared to 60 percent of white males and 62 percent of student athletes overall. The averages across four cohorts of basketball players were 39 percent and 52 percent for black men and white men, respectively. Forty-seven percent of black male football players graduated within six years, compared to 63 percent of their white teammates. Harper's findings led to this conclusion: "Perhaps nowhere in higher education is the disenfranchisement of black male students more insidious than in college athletics" (p. 6).

In addition to these quantifiable racial gaps in degree attainment, more than twenty-five years ago Edwards (1984) observed about black sports participants: "They must contend, of course, with the connotations and social reverberations of the traditional 'dumb jock' caricature. But Black student-athletes are burdened also with the insidiously racist implications of the myth of 'innate Black athletic superiority,' and the more blatantly racist stereotype of the 'dumb Negro' condemned by racial heritage to intellectual inferiority" (p. 8). More recently, Benson (2000) found that many black males are socialized to prioritize sports over academics when they are in high school, and such messages are sustained (and arguably amplified) once they enroll in college. In an article in the *Chronicle of Higher Education* titled "Black Athletes and White Professors: A Twilight Zone of Uncertainty," black male student athletes reported feeling that they were not taken seriously by many of their white professors (Perlmutter, 2003). Related to this, Comeaux and Harrison (2007) found that engagement with faculty, particularly outside the classroom, was essential to academic achievement for black and white male student athletes alike, but professors devoted significantly more time to academic engagement with white student athletes.

Although much of the existing literature on black male student athletes in Division I sports programs at four-year institutions explores the social construction of their athletic identities, their lived experiences with racial stereotyping and low expectations, and one specific outcome variable (bachelor's degree completion), these topics remain largely unexplored in the context of community college sports. In fact, Harris and Harper (2008) contend that most of what has been published about male community college students narrowly pertains to how many enroll, earn an associate degree, and transfer. Little emphasis has been placed on demonstrated institutional commitment to the overall success of black male students, particularly those who play on sports teams at community colleges. Thus the purpose of this chapter is to consider the mutual benefits that could accrue for these students and the colleges they attend if the transfer rate to four-year institutions is strengthened. Although transferring to a four-year college or university is the outcome variable of interest here, I certainly recognize the importance of examining learning and other developmental outcomes; this is something I hope to see in future scholarship on black male community college student athletes. I later explain why I chose to focus expressly on transferring to the four-year as an outcome. Critical Race Theory, specifically the Interest Convergence tenet, is introduced in the next section and used for explanatory sense making throughout the chapter.

Critical Race Theory and Interest Convergence

Based on scholarly perspectives from law, sociology, history, ethnic studies, and women's studies, Critical Race Theory (CRT) is a conceptual lens used to examine racism, racial (dis)advantages, and inequitable distribution of power and privilege within institutions and society (Bell, 1987; Delgado and Stefancic, 2001). CRT also challenges misconceptions regarding colorblindness, merit, and racial equity; critiques the presumed innocence of self-proclaimed white liberals; and ignites consciousness that leads to social justice and advances for people of color (Crenshaw, Gotanda, Peller, and Thomas, 1995). According to Donnor (2005), CRT offers an especially useful lens through which "to better recognize and more fully understand the forces that have constructed a system in which African American male athletes are cheered on the field by wealthy alumni and powerful fans while at the same time denied opportunities to earn the degree that could lead to wealth and power of their own" (p. 63).

One major tenet of CRT is Interest Convergence, which, according to Delgado (1995), typically compels white people to advocate for the advancement of people of color only if their own self-interest is better served. Put differently, theorists posit that those in the majority who enact social, political, and economic change on behalf of minorities rarely do so without first identifying the personal costs and gains associated with such actions. This perspective is informed by the Marxist theory that the bourgeoisie will work toward progress for the proletariat only if advances ultimately end up benefitting the bourgeoisie more (Taylor, 2006). It is certainly not our intent to liken community colleges to "the bourgeoisie," but we do argue that many white college faculty, administrators, and coaches must be made aware of the overall benefit to the institution (and in some instances, to themselves) before moving forward a serious strategic agenda to improve educational outcomes for black male student athletes. Hence, Interest Convergence is used in this chapter to help answer the question, Why would a community college whose faculty and staff is majority white deliberately engage in efforts to strengthen the rate at which its black male student athletes transfer to four-year institutions?

Delgado and Stefancic (2001) argue that prior attempts to eradicate racism and racial differences in social, educational, and economic outcomes have produced minimal results because of insufficient convergence of interests. As Bell writes, "We cannot ignore and should learn from and try to recognize situations when there is a convergence of interests" (2000, p. 9). Making clear how transferring more black male student athletes to four-year institutions will ultimately increase the overall transfer rate for the community college is one example; I say more about this later. Another is pointing out how the prevailing culture of the college would benefit from having

NEW DIRECTIONS FOR COMMUNITY COLLEGES • DOI: 10.1002/cc

black male sports participants—those who are often among the most visible students on campus (Person and LeNoir, 1997)—model for their peers (other student athletes and nonathletes alike) a serious disposition toward academic achievement.

In the Common Interest of Transferring

I have identified transferring from community college to a four-year institution as an important intersecting point of interest. For many (but certainly not all) black male student athletes, the opportunity to play their chosen sport on a bigger and more competitive field or court is appealing. Thus aspirations of transferring to a four-year college or university are more common than not for this group. These aspirations are in many ways connected to longer-term goals of playing professional sports. Donnor (2005) indicates: "Black males participating in sports are more likely to possess aspirations for pursuing sports professionally than their white counterparts because they believe they will be treated fairly. As a result, African American males will generally interpret their involvement in intercollegiate (and interscholastic) sports as a conduit for achieving their career aspirations" (p. 48).

Rudman (1986) found that blacks were more likely than whites to aspire to a career in professional sports. He suggested this difference in sport orientation is a result of social structures (for example, racism) that limit opportunities for blacks in other professional occupations. According to a 2006 NCAA report, 1.8 percent of college football players are drafted by the National Football League (NFL) and 1.2 percent of men's college basketball players are drafted by the National Basketball Association (NBA). Although these odds are generally well known, many black male student athletes, including those at community colleges, exert tremendous effort to render themselves competitive for professional sports drafts. Transferring to a four-year institution makes actualization of professional sports aspirations considerably more likely; this is something that many black male community college athletes understand and work toward.

Similarly, transferring students to four-year institutions is a publicly stated goal and core function of most community colleges. Transfer readiness and the actual transfer rate remain among the most widely studied topics in the community college literature (Pascarella and Terenzini, 2005). However, because of a number of structural, financial, and informational barriers, only a small proportion of community college students who intend to transfer to a four-year institution actually do so (Advisory Committee on Student Financial Assistance, 2008; Long, 2005). Even when students' goals are transfer-oriented, many end up ineligible or insufficiently prepared to transfer (Hagedorn and others, 2006; Laanan, 2003). Previous research has found that the transfer rate is especially low among racial and ethnic minorities and low-income students. For example, Hagedorn and others (2006) note, "Students of color and those from low-income backgrounds are disproportionately impacted by the sluggish nature of transfer, because the majority of these students who go to college will begin their postsecondary education in community colleges" (p. 224). Notwithstanding this area of institutional underperformance, transferring more students to four-year institutions remains among the major priorities for community colleges— one for which accountability agents are demanding increased effectiveness, as enrollments are beginning to reach capacity at many public four-year institutions and states are relying more on community colleges to offer the first stage of postsecondary education for students (Long, 2005).

Despite this goal in common between student athletes and community colleges, black men transfer at a low rate, especially in comparison to their white male peers. We recently discovered racial disparities in transfer rate among student athletes at several community colleges. For example, Pima Community College District in Arizona transferred 17 percent of its black male football players, in comparison to 63 percent of their white teammates, to four-year institutions in 2008. Similar trends were found in men's basketball programs at Dixie State College in Utah (25 versus 56 percent), Enterprise-Ozark Community College in Alabama (25 versus 50 percent), and Gadsden State Community College in Georgia (0 versus 67 percent), to name a few. Data from these four institutions and several others make clear that transfer as a shared outcome of interest among many black male student athletes and the community colleges they attend has not effectively converged.

What's in It for the College?

In my view, the Interest Convergence tenet of CRT has at least one noteworthy limitation. It presumes that white persons rarely do anything "out of the good-ness of the heart" that advantages people of color. Accepting this as an absolute truth would be shortsighted. I acknowledge that there are white community college faculty, staff, and coaches who care authentically about minority stu-dent success. Indeed, some colleagues are committed for reasons that extend beyond their own selfish profits (educational and otherwise). However, I still find perspectives on Interest Convergence useful; there are some white com-munity college professionals who will need to clearly see the ultimate value in deliberately constructing an educational environment that increases the trans-fer rate specifically for black male student athletes. Some may not easily rec-ognize how their individual efforts might ultimately benefit the college overall, not just one segment of the student body (black males). Therefore, in this sec-tion I offer four ways in which community colleges would benefit from trans-ferring a larger number of black male student athletes to four-year institutions.

First, when the transfer rate for black male student athletes increases, so too does the overall transfer rate for the college. This is especially true at community colleges where a disproportionate number of black male stu-dents play on sports teams. Given the dismal transfer rate for community college students in general (Laanan, 2003; Long, 2005) and students of color in particular (Hagedorn and others, 2006), every individual black male student who transfers could make a potentially noticeable contribution to an institution's overall rate. In this era of increased transparency and accountability, institutions are expected to furnish evidence on the production of key educational outcomes (U.S. Department of Education, 2006). For community colleges, transferring students to four-year institutions is among the areas in which accountability agents expect to see progress. Thus, closing the gap between black male student athletes and their white teammates would ultimately fortify the college's efforts to confirm its educational effectiveness.

Increasing the number of black male student athletes who transfer to four-year institutions would also result in reputational gains for the community college. Harper and Hurtado (2007) found that some institutions garner a reputation within minority communities for being racist, which negatively affects student recruitment. Black and Latino participants in the study reported that family members discouraged their interest in certain predominantly white institutions because they were known to maintain a toxic campus racial climate and had long been ineffective in fostering an enabling environment for minority student success. As a community college helps more black male student athletes actualize their goal of transferring to a four-year institution, its reputation for doing so will improve. This could potentially compel talented prospective student athletes to more strongly consider one particular college over others. For example, if a prospective black male basketball player knows a certain community college does an outstanding job of helping members of the basketball team transfer to four-year institutions with excellent basketball programs, he would likely be more inclined to apply, enroll, and play basketball at that community college. Attracting more student athletes who choose an institution for this reason could also create a transfer culture on community college sports teams.

Third, coaches who work at a community college where the president holds educators and administrators uncompromisingly accountable for student success also have much to gain from enacting efforts to increase the transfer rate among black male student athletes. Benson (2000) found that coaches were complicit in the academic underperformance of black male student athletes. In fact, coaches often conveyed to these students that athletics were more important than academics. Community college leaders must expect athletics departments to furnish evidence of their contribution to the institution's transfer mission. If compensation and reappointment of coaches were based not only on wins and losses but also on transfer and graduation rates, then those who work most closely with student athletes would have more incentive to ensure their success. In the absence of accountability from the president, district leaders, and other top administrators, athletics departments will continue to help manufacture racial gaps in the transfer rate like those we cited earlier in this chapter. Seventy percent of the former black male student athletes who participated in Beamon's study (2008) also had careers of varying length in professional sports. These men reported being made to feel like "used goods" by the colleges and universities at which they had been student athletes. For sure, such feelings are unlikely to incite these alumni to contribute financially to their alma mater.

Finally, community colleges should recognize that student athletes who transfer to four-year institutions could eventually be among the 1.2 percent drafted by NBA or the 1.8 percent drafted by the NFL. Once their professional sports careers become lucrative, these black male alumni could be solicited for donations to the college. It is possible that some for whom the community college served as the springboard into sports participation at a four-year institution and subsequently into professional athletics may be easily persuaded to support the college's development endeavors. Long (2005) asserts, "Even as their role increases and their transfer function grows in importance, community colleges are facing reductions in funding" (p. 2). Given this, community colleges would benefit from expanding their revenue sources to include donations from alumni (Jenkins and Glass, 1999). It is possible that the wealthiest former students may be those who transferred to a four-year institution and later secured a multimillion dollar contract to play on a professional sports team.

Conclusion

I offered just four examples of how community colleges and their athletics departments and coaches would benefit from increasing the transfer rate among black male student athletes. These reasons were not meant to replace other more altruistic motives, such as an authentic commitment to racial equity, improving the transfer rate for the sake of mission realization, or investing in actualization of all students' aspirations and success. I recognize these as most important. However, persistent disparities in transfer rate between black men and their white male counterparts signify to us that few educators, administrators, and coaches are likely to participate in strategic closing of a racialized outcome gap if the tangible return on their personal investment is not made more apparent. Regardless of the impetus, current transfer rates make clear that considerably more effort is required to improve black male student athlete transfers from community colleges to four-year institutions. Necessary and important are increased transparency and accountability, more research expressly focused on race and community college athletics, and the effective convergence of black male student athletes' interests with those of the community colleges they attend.

References

Adler, P., and Adler, P. A. "Role Conflict and Identity Salience: College Athletics and the Academic Role." *Social Science Journal*, 1987, 24(4), 443–455.

NEW DIRECTIONS FOR COMMUNITY COLLEGES • DOI: 10.1002/cc

Advisory Committee on Student Financial Assistance. *Transition Matters: Community College to Bachelor's Degree.* Washington, D.C.: Advisory Committee on Student Financial Assistance, 2008.

Beamon, K. K. "Used Goods: Former African American College Student-Athlete's Perception of Exploitation by Division I Universities." *Journal of Negro Education,* 2008, 77(4), 352–364.

Bell, D. A. *And We Are Not Saved: The Elusive Quest for Racial Justice.* New York: Basic Books, 1987.

Bell, D. A. *"Brown vs. Board of Education:* Forty-Five Years After the Fact." *Ohio Northern Law Review,* 2000, 26(2), 171–182.

Benson, K. F. "Constructing Academic Inadequacy: African-American Athletes' Stories." *Journal of Higher Education,* 2000, 71(2), 223–246.

Comeaux, E., and Harrison C. K. "Faculty and Male Student Athletes: Racial Differences in the Environmental Predictors of Academic Achievement." *Race, Ethnicity and Education,* 2007, 10, 199–214.

Crenshaw, K., Gotanda, N., Peller, G., and Thomas, K. (eds.). *Critical Race Theory: The Key Writings That Formed the Movement.* New York: New Press, 1995.

Delgado, R. *Critical Race Theory: The Cutting Edge.* Philadelphia: Temple University Press, 1995.

Delgado, R., and Stefancic, J. *Critical Race Theory: An Introduction.* New York: New York University Press, 2001.

Donnor, J. K. "Towards an Interest-Convergence in the Education of African American Football Student-Athletes in Major College Sports." *Race, Ethnicity and Education,* 2005, 8(1), 45–67.

Edwards, H. "The Black 'Dumb Jock': An American Sports Tragedy." *College Board Review,* 1984, 131, 8–13.

Gaston-Gayles, J. "Examining Academic and Athletic Motivation Among Student Athletes at a Division I University." *Journal of College Student Development,* 2004, 45(1), 75–83.

Hagedorn, L. S., Moon, H. S., Cypers, S., Maxwell, W. E., and Lester, J. "Transfer Between Community Colleges and Four-Year Colleges: The All-American Game." *Community College Journal of Research and Practice,* 2006, 30(3), 223–242.

Harper, S. R. *Black Male Students at Public Universities in the U.S.: Status, Trends and Implications for Policy and Practice.* Washington, D.C.: Joint Center for Political and Economic Studies, 2006.

Harper, S. R., and Hurtado, S. "Nine Themes in Campus Racial Climates and Implications for Institutional Transformation." In S. R. Harper and L. D. Patton (eds.), *Responding to the Realities of Race on Campus.* New Directions for Student Services, no. 120. San Francisco: Jossey-Bass, 2007.

Harris, F., III, and Harper, S. R. "Masculinities Go to Community College: Understanding Male Identity Socialization and Gender Role Conflict." In J. Lester (ed.), *Gendered Perspectives in Community Colleges.* New Directions for Community Colleges, no. 142. San Francisco: Jossey-Bass, 2008.

Jenkins, L. W., and Glass, C. J. "Inception, Growth, and Development of a Community College Foundation: Lessons to Be Learned." *Community College Journal of Research and Practice,* 1999, 23(6), 593–612.

Laanan, F. S. "Degree Aspirations of Two-Year College Students." *Community College Journal of Research and Practice,* 2003, 27(6), 495–518.

Long, B. T. *State Financial Aid: Policies to Enhance Articulation and Transfer.* Boulder, Colo.: Western Interstate Commission for Higher Education, 2005.

Martin, B. E. "Redefining Championship in College Sports: Enhancing Outcomes and Increasing Student-Athlete Engagement." In S. R. Harper and S. J. Quaye (eds.), *Student Engagement in Higher Education: Theoretical Perspectives and Practical Approaches for Diverse Populations.* New York: Routledge, 2009.

Martin, B. E., and Harris, F., III. "Examining Productive Conceptions of Masculinities: Lessons Learned from Academically Driven African American Male Student-Athletes." *Journal of Men's Studies,* 2006, *14*(3), 359–378.

Messer, K. L. "African American Male College Athletes." In M. J. Cuyjet (ed.), *African American Men in College.* San Francisco: Jossey-Bass, 2006.

Miller, P. S., and Kerr, G. "The Athletic Academic and Social Experiences of Intercollegiate Student-Athletes." *Journal of Sport Behavior,* 2002, *25*(4), 346–365.

National Collegiate Athletic Association. *Report on Careers in Professional Sports.* Indianapolis: NCAA, 2006.

Parham, W. D. "The Intercollegiate Athlete: A 1990s Profile." *Counseling Psychologist,* 1993, *21*(3), 411–429.

Pascarella, E. T., and Smart, J. C. "Impact of Intercollegiate Athletic Participation for African American and Caucasian Men: Some Further Evidence." *Journal of College Student Development,* 1991, *32*(2), 123–130.

Pascarella, E. T., and Terenzini, P. T. *How College Affects Students, Vol. 2: A Third Decade of Research.* San Francisco: Jossey-Bass, 2005.

Pascarella, E. T., Truckenmiller, R., Nora, A., Terenzini, P. T., Edison, M., and Hagedorn, L. S. "Cognitive Impacts of Intercollegiate Athletics Participation: Some Further Evidence." *Journal of Higher Education,* 1999, *70*(1), 1–26.

Perlmutter, D. "Black Athletes and White Professor: A Twilight Zone of Uncertainty." *Chronicle of Higher Education,* 2003, B7–B9.

Person, D. R., and LeNoir, K. M. "Retention Issues and Models for African American Male Athletes." In M. J. Cuyjet (ed.), *Helping African American Men Succeed in College. New Directions for Student Services,* no. 80. San Francisco: Jossey-Bass, 1997.

Pinkerton, R. S., Hinz, L. D., and Barrow, J. C. "The College Student-Athlete: Psychological Considerations and Interventions." *Journal of American College Health,* 1989, *37*(5), 218–225.

Rudman, W. J. "The Sport Mystique in Black Culture." *Sociology of Sport Journal,* 1986, *3*(4), 305–319.

Sedlacek, W. E., and Adams-Gaston, J. "Predicting the Academic Success of Student-Athletes Using SAT and Non-Cognitive Variables." *Journal of Counseling and Development,* 1992, *70*(6), 724–727.

Simons, H. D., Van Rheenen, D., and Covington, M. V. "Academic Motivation and the Student-Athlete." *Journal of College Student Development,* 1999, *40*(2), 151–162.

Taylor, E. "A Critical Race Analysis of the Achievement Gap in the United States: Politics, Reality, and Hope." *Leadership and Policy in Schools,* 2006, *5*(1), 71–87.

U.S. Department of Education. *A Test of Leadership: Charting the Future of U.S. Higher Education. A Report of the Commission Appointed by Secretary of Education Margaret Spellings.* Washington, D.C.: U.S. Department of Education, 2006.

SHAUN R. HARPER is assistant professor of higher education management at the University of Pennsylvania. He also holds a faculty appointment in the Center for Africana Studies at Penn.

4

This chapter presents pertinent topics for institutional leaders to consider in developing and maintaining a community college athletic program. The authors present a "road map" for institutional decision makers involved in expanding, eliminating, or maintaining athletic teams and programs.

Considerations for Expanding, Eliminating, and Maintaining Community College Athletic Teams and Programs

Heather J. Lawrence, Christopher M. Mullin, David Horton, Jr.

Collegiate athletic programs have often been referred to as the "front porch" of an institution (Nazarian, 2007). Coaches, athletic teams, student athletes, and athletic department staff serve as a "link between the immediate campus family and the larger community" (p. 4). It is this front-porch principle that makes managing intercollegiate athletics a unique and challenging endeavor. This chapter gives community college leaders and decision makers a road map for handling situations regarding expansion, elimination, or continued maintenance of athletic teams and programs at their institution.

Every year, community college athletic programs have an impact on more than seventy-eight thousand student athletes through sponsorship of some two dozen men's and women's individual and team sports at more than 630 institutions in the United States and Canada (Commission on Athletics, n.d.; National Junior College Athletic Association, 2008; Northwest Athletic Association of Community Colleges, n.d.). The presence of an athletic program at the community college can generate a sense of belonging, boost student morale and alumni support, increase retention, and positively affect student athletes' academic success (Ashburn, 2007; Berson, 1996; Rishe, 2003). It is for these reasons that athletics at the community college

NEW DIRECTIONS FOR COMMUNITY COLLEGES, no. 147, Fall 2009 © 2009 Wiley Periodicals, Inc.
Published online in Wiley InterScience (www.interscience.wiley.com) • DOI: 10.1002/cc.376

is often considered an important part of the authentic collegiate experience. Given the influence of athletics at postsecondary institutions, the lack of available scholarly and best-practice literature regarding matters related specifically to community college athletics is surprising and may even be termed alarming.

The vast majority of literature related to athletics is focused on NCAA Division I and Division II institutions and their issues. Because the NCAA does not have a category of membership for two-year institutions, community colleges have been overlooked with respect to research. Therefore, the existing literature has yet to adequately address issues related to athletics and student athletes specifically enrolled in community colleges (Horton, 2009). The need for further discussion and scholarly exploration was recently discussed in a study by Williams, Byrd, and Pennington (2008), which examined athletics at the community college and the process for establishing or expanding athletic programs. The study suggested that "over 70 percent of college presidents were not fully aware of the process for establishing an athletic program or adding athletic teams at their college" (p. 457).

Accordingly, this and other chapters in this issue offer a framework with which institutional leaders can increase their understanding and knowledge of issues concerning athletics and student athletes at the community college. Specifically, with reference to the community college, this chapter (1) examines community college athletics from a historical perspective, (2) discusses the role of athletics within the context of institutional mission, and (3) discusses some primary and secondary factors to consider in making decisions regarding expansion, elimination, or maintenance of an athletic program.

History and Governance of Community College Athletics

There are currently three major governing bodies overseeing intercollegiate athletics at community colleges in the United States and Canada (two regional and one national): the Commission on Athletics (COA), the Northwest Athletic Association of Community Colleges (NWAACC), and the National Junior College Athletic Association (NJCAA).

According to the COA, community college athletic competition can be traced back to 1929, when the California Junior College Federation (currently known as COA) was formed. Since that time, the COA has been the only governing entity administering intercollegiate athletics rules and policies statewide in California. The COA currently governs athletic programs and athletic competitions for 103 institutions in the state. It is authorized by the state legislature, which has given the organization governing authority over all of the California system community colleges and the more than twenty-five thousand student athletes in the system (Commission on Athletics, n.d.).

Formerly known as the Washington State Junior College Athletic Conference, the NWAACC oversees athletic competitions for its thirty-six member institutions located in Washington State, Oregon, and Vancouver, B.C. Operating since 1946, the NWAACC has been sponsoring league and national championship events in football, basketball, baseball, tennis, track, and golf (Northwest Athletic Association of Community Colleges, n.d.). Unlike the COA, the NWAAC does not operate under legislative authority, thus creating a more diverse membership that crosses state and international borders.

In 1938, the NJCAA was founded by a group of thirteen junior colleges in California. One of the first events sponsored by the newly established organization was the 1939 National Junior College Track and Field Meet in Sacramento (National Junior College Athletic Association, n.d.; Reapple, Peery, and Hohman, 1982). Since the late 1950s, the NJCAA has been considered the largest national governing body for athletics at public, accredited community colleges. More than fifty-one thousand students participated in athletics at NJCAA member institutions during the 2007–08 academic year (National Junior College Athletic Association, n.d.). Member institutions are divided into twenty-four regions, with separate men's and women's regional directors (National Junior College Athletic Association, n.d.).

The benefits of membership vary with the governing body. The governing organizations furnish a structured environment in which intercollegiate athletic competition can thrive. These organizations establish and enforce minimum academic standards for student and institutional participation; enforce sport competition rules and regulations; financially support postseason and championship competitions; and annually award team, individual, and institutional recognition. The variety of governing associations and the loose configuration of community college athletics give institutions the opportunity to develop an athletic program that can align with institutional missions and priorities. The NCAA and many four-year institutions (although not all four-year institutions are NCAA members) have a much more regulated governance structure.

The Purpose of Athletics at the Community College

The community college was developed to offer educational opportunities beyond high school to a broad spectrum of students, including those who are place-bound in the community or cannot afford postsecondary education away from home (Cohen and Brawer, 2008; Gleazer, 1980). Twenty-five states currently allocate local tax support to community colleges (Dowd and Grant, 2006), thereby reinforcing local stakeholders' ownership in and responsibility for the well-being of the institution.

Ideally, athletics at the community college is integral to the educational process and complements the mission of the institution (Horton, 2009; Reapple, Peery, and Hohman, 1982). Many of the problems faced by NCAA athletics programs—commercialization, excess spending, and rules violations—can be associated with institutions losing sight of the primary reason athletics is a component of the educational experience (Duderstadt, 2003;

Sperber, 2000). A recent study of community college presidents' perceptions of athletics revealed that many respondents at institutions with athletic teams agreed that athletics supports the mission of the college (Williams and Pennington, 2006). Just as presidential leadership is imperative to students' academic success, it is also crucial for athletic success. The support and promotion of athletics as a valuable co-curricular activity on the part of institutional leaders is vital to a thriving, sustainable athletic program.

Community college missions often entail promoting educational opportunities to a local population. When attempting to align an athletic program with this type of mission, some challenges may occur. One community college president noted during the 2007–08 academic year that only one of the forty-one student athletes living on campus came from within their service district. Because the athletic program was not supporting the institutional purpose, it was dissolved in May 2008 by the president and board of trustees. Other factors leading to elimination of the program were (1) overall operating and personnel costs, (2) high costs associated with baseball and softball field maintenance, (3) the long-term savings supplied by discontinuing foodservice and on-campus residence hall operations, (4) lack of local support for the athletic program, and (5) low student-athlete graduation rate. The cost savings are projected to be redirected to attract local students through new academic degree and certificate programs, hire new staff, and establish new scholarships to attract local and minority students. Although the decision by the president and board to eliminate athletics was controversial, "it was made with the best interest of the entire institution in mind" (interview with "Bill Elliot," pseudonym, Mar. 28, 2008).

In recent years, a number of community colleges have dropped athletic programs at their institution for purely financial reasons. One college in particular, located in the southern region of the United States, eliminated its athletics program in 2001 because of projected state budget cuts. The athletic program was later partially reinstated in 2005 following arrival of a new president (McLellan, 2001; interview with Nancy Keenum, Jan. 30, 2008). Reinstatement of the institution's baseball and softball teams resulted in approximately fifty new full-time enrolled students (a mix of local and regional students) attending the institution the following year (Keenum interview, 2008). Examining the impact of athletics on the local economy, one community college administrator observed that student athletes rent housing from the community and patronize local businesses (Keenum interview, 2008). This results in additional economic impact on the locale, which ultimately benefits the institution and community.

Considerations for adding, eliminating, or maintaining an athletic program or athletic teams can present a number of challenges. An institution seeking to add or eliminate an athletic program or teams needs first to prepare a plan that is transparent to stakeholders. The plan should clearly communicate how addition or elimination of the program complements the core ideologies of the institution. This communication should emphasize how offering athletics aligns with the institution's mission and purpose.

Preparing a plan of action requires careful consideration on the part of the governing board, president, and other institutional leaders, because there are a number of factors to consider. Given the impact a major change in athletics can have on the institution, formal approval should come from highest authority possible, in most cases a governing board. For the purpose of this discussion, these challenges and trade-offs have been divided into primary and secondary considerations. The next section examines some primary considerations, consisting of issues that are generally associated with sponsorship of an athletic program at a community college.

Primary Considerations for Athletics Operations

Operating an athletic program is expensive and challenging, especially in the current environment of steadily declining state financial support for public higher education. Generally speaking, athletic programs are not directly supported through state funding formulas, as are some other units and agencies on campus. For example, although Alabama supplies funds for athletically related financial aid for community college student athletes, most states do not give institutions funds specifically for athletic purposes. Thus institutions are forced to rely completely on their ability to self-generate revenue to cover athletic expenses.

State and Local Support

Approximately forty states use some type of funding formula in allocating state funds to public institutions. All of these formulas take into account full-time equivalent students or student headcount in allocating funds (Mullin and Honeyman, 2007). Though there is no empirical evidence showing a definite link between athletics and increased enrollment at the community college, there is general agreement among scholars and practitioners that athletics is a factor in increasing enrollment at rural-serving community colleges (Castañeda, Katsinas, and Hardy, 2006) and other areas of the country where sports may attract more local students and student athletes (Ashburn, 2007; Williams and Pennington, 2006). For example, one eastern community college started women's soccer and volleyball and men's basketball and baseball to attract more local and out-of-state students (Ashburn, 2007). The impact of athletics on state funding will ultimately enter into state funding through formulas related to student enrollment. It may be argued, then, that an increase in student athletes could result in greater state support.

It is of course not recommended that institutions rely solely on tax-generated revenue to support athletic programs; given the unrestricted nature of these funds they may be redirected to other programs thanks to the competing interests of faculty and administrators at the institution. For example, if an institution has "winning" programs, then local and state support may be directed to reinforce continued success, and the discretionary nature of the funds may place academics secondary to athletics. To ensure the fiscal stability of an athletic program, and to limit concern that athletics detracts from a focus on academics at the institution, support for athletics might best be garnered via fundraising, community outreach, and service-learning opportunities for local student athletes.

Generating Revenue

Athletic programs may be supported by several sources, among them the traditional revenue streams of state government, local government, and student fees. However, creating new entrepreneurial revenue sources is becoming a requirement to keep pace with escalating operational costs. Levin (2000) found that community college behaviors have begun to resemble those of private business and industry in moving toward more reliance on the private sector for funding. Athletics has followed this model with respect to increased reliance on private sector funding. Administrators and coaches are being challenged to self-generate athletic budgets as opposed to being given allocations from the institution. In developing a plan of action to add an athletic program or teams, it is important to identify sustainable short-term and long-term plans for generating revenues to support the program (fundraising, corporate partnerships, student fees).

Fundraising. Community colleges have been considered nontraditional among the various types of institutions of higher education. Characteristics that describe them best include adaptive and entrepreneurial (Cohen and Brawer, 2008). Entrepreneurial institutions are those able to garner additional revenues from governmental programs or through private markets (Dowd and Grant, 2007) to financially sustain the institution. Developing an entrepreneurial identity may be necessary to support an institution's athletics program. Colleges can approach this in many ways. A common procedure is to allocate resources to each athletic team for basic necessities such as coaching, league or conference fees, and travel, uniforms, and scholarships (specific to scholarship-granting institutions). Coaches and teams are often responsible for generating monies for expenses and activities that extend beyond these areas such as travel to additional tournaments, training trips, team activities, and extra team gear. Additionally, fundraising programs or campaigns are an effective way to increase local support and alumni involvement.

Leveraging relationships with former student athletes is another way to encourage alumni support as well as generate revenue. Identifying former students and student athletes to assist the institution in raising private funds can alleviate some of the financial pressures of supporting athletic teams. For instance, organizing games pitting current student athletes against alumni may foster a connection between current and former student athletes, as well as reconnect alumni to the institution. Community colleges may take advantage of alumni participation to solicit donations and gifts. Beyond the possible donations that may come from events such as alumni games, the informal networking that occurs (that is, potential jobs for current student athletes) during such events can be extremely valuable to current students.

Corporate Partnerships. Corporate partnerships are often thought of as being an option only for big-time college sports programs. In reality, many local businesses, especially those that directly benefit from the college, can prove to be a financial asset to an athletic program and its teams. For example, a women's basketball team might partner with a local restaurant by directing visiting teams to the establishment (via coupons) in exchange for short-term or long-term financial sponsorships. This type of arrangement may be an easy way for businesses to see value because it can be directly measured by cash receipts from visiting teams and out-of-town spectators.

Activity Fees and Ancillaries. Student activity fees and ancillary revenues can also support athletic operations. Depending on state regulations, institutions may increase student activity fees to support the athletic program. However, caution must be taken in considering any rise in student tuition costs, because this may be in direct conflict with the mission of the institution. Other revenue-generating sources to consider are game admission fees, concessions, event parking, advertising (signage and uniforms), and sale of athletic paraphernalia at the institution's bookstore to augment existing sources of revenue. Increasing student fees is a long-term solution, but the other presented options are only a temporary or short-term fix; revenues generated from these sources depend hugely on local support.

Athletic Scholarships. Whether to offer athletic scholarships or not depends on the college's circumstances and mission. However, administrators should not assume that scholarships must always be offered to ensure a successful athletic program. Many students value the opportunity to participate in athletics beyond high school as sufficient reward. Horton discussed the value and personal benefit associated with athletic participation in an earlier chapter of this volume. He noted that these benefits may be especially valuable for those students who remain close to home to meet their academic, athletic, and personal needs. Institutions may also consider offering partial scholarships as a way of containing costs while still presenting an incentive for students to attend and play sports at their institution. Though many successful athletic programs do award athletic scholarships, it is also possible to have a solid program without providing student athletes with athletically related financial aid.

Facilities. Although it would be desirable to have a sparkling new facility for all athletic teams, the cost of building such facilities is prohibitive for most institutions. A first step is for administrators and coaches to work with existing local facilities to secure sites for in-season competition and scheduled practices. This may involve additional cost to the athletic program in the form of rental or shared maintenance fees.

Regardless of whether an institution constructs a new facility or uses an existing facility for the athletic teams, the facilities must be gender-equitable. Thus the men's basketball team cannot negotiate with a neighboring NCAA Division I institution to use its new gym and while the women's team practices at a local recreation center that is in a state of disrepair. A plan for facilities use should be an ongoing part of athletic operations. With respect to new construction or renovation, strategies that adopt a phased approach usually are most sensible and are probably more feasible within available budgets.

Maintenance costs associated with ownership of both indoor and outdoor athletic centers should be examined carefully. Competitive athletic programs require a great deal of attention to facility preparation, which may not fit within the existing job descriptions or expertise of maintenance personnel. Outdoor fields must be mowed, watered, and frequently tended to, while indoor facilities must be sanitized, set up, and broken down for practice and competition. Use and maintenance of athletic facilities is an expense that can be managed, but it cannot be eliminated.

Travel. Important aspects of sports are the camaraderie and development of students that occur on the road as they travel for competition. Nonetheless, the socioemotional benefits of travel need to be balanced against the costs. Costs are to be seen as both financial to the institution and in missed class time for students.

Arranging team travel is but another major operational expense for an athletic program. Travel expenses can vary substantially according to the region in which the institution is located. Some regions have a concentrated population of participating colleges, which makes for minimal travel for competition, while institutions in other regions may be required to travel a significant distance to compete. A key in managing travel costs is offering sports that are also sponsored by other institutions in the region. The further and more frequently a team has to travel to compete, the more costly it becomes.

Missed class time should also be kept to a minimum for students and considered in scheduling competitions. Competing in tournaments is an excellent way to engage in competition without traveling to multiple sites. For those schools with proper facilities, personnel, and local lodging, hosting tournaments with multiple teams can save money and even potentially generate additional revenue. If available, college-owned transportation can be a cost-effective mode of transportation, and many community colleges have already invested in buses that may sit idle for much of the year.

Equipment. The safety of the student athlete should be the institution's first priority. All protective gear should be inspected at regular intervals by qualified specialists and refurbished as needed. Many companies now offer refurbishing or reconditioning of equipment and sell used equipment that is certified safe. Costs can be reduced by using reconditioning services, as opposed to buying new equipment every year.

Institutions cannot avoid purchasing safety equipment or team competition uniforms, but uniforms can be used for multiple seasons as long as they are kept in good repair. Practice gear can be generic in style and look, or students can be asked to furnish their own safe and appropriate practice wear. Athletic shoes can also be a large expense for the institution. This is an area in which an institution can take advantage of an opportunity to build a relationship with a local sporting goods store to supply specialty shoes for the institution's student athletes. In the best situation, the store would become a sponsor and donate equipment in exchange for advertising on the uniforms or other benefits. If that is not an option, the school might be able to get shoes for a reduced rate, subsequently setting up an account for each student athlete. The store may then assist the student athletes individually with their athletic gear needs. The student athletes will probably buy some other gear while getting their shoes (or spend more than their allocation on their shoes), thus generating new revenue for the store and justifying the partnership with the school.

Salaries. One benefit that community college athletic programs enjoy over other types of schools is the ability for faculty and staff to take on multiple roles on campus. It is commonplace to find an existing faculty member with expertise and interest in coaching a sport team. Various models exist for funding community college coaching salaries. Some institutions give course releases to faculty who also coach an athletic team, thus minimizing direct cost to the athletic department. In most cases, however, some funding must be available to compensate coaches, whether they are existing employees or not. Institutions must be clear in identifying whether the primary role of the employee is "coach" or "faculty." This will help to avoid instances in which underperformance in one aspect of the job puts the entire job at risk. In addition to funds for coaches' salaries, further resources may need to be allocated for athletic support staff.

Naming an athletics director is paramount to the organizational success of the athletic program. It is very tempting to assume that a single coach or coaches can collectively run the athletic department, but this situation must be avoided whenever possible. The business and administrative skills needed to manage the program are very different from the skill set required to be a successful coach. Another trap that should also be avoided is that of using salary to compete for "the best" coaches and administrators. If athletics is truly offered to enhance the education of the students involved, then institutions must be willing to seek out qualified coaches within their available budgetary limitations and according to the intended goals of the athletic program.

Secondary Considerations for Athletics Operations.

There are certain costs inherent to sponsoring an athletics program that cannot be eliminated or cut. However, with creativity and some hard work, revenues can be maximized and expenses managed so that athletics can be a vital part of the institution without being a financial drain. Every institution has its own financial management and its own overall budgeting priorities. We consider the factors presented here to be secondary in nature but still worthy of discussion.

Recruitment and Retention. Depending on the institution's location and intended goals for the athletic program, recruiting may or may not be taxing or even necessary. In areas with popular high school sports programs, attracting student athletes may simply involve establishing relationships with local high school players and coaches. In some instances, more extensive recruiting might be necessary to fill certain positions on the team, but efforts should be made to recruit locally and regionally whenever possible in concert with the local mission of the community college. This will also control costs through limited traveling for recruiting-related activities. Undoubtedly, many community college coaches will be juggling coaching, teaching, and other responsibilities, so it is important to have expectations in recruiting that take into account their other obligations.

Efforts to bring athletes to the institution should be matched with efforts to help the athlete persist toward academic goals. Including staff from academic affairs in the planning and maintenance of an athletic program is paramount to maintaining the academic mission of the institution. To best serve student athletes, identifying and including a limited number of academic affairs staff as part of an athletic-academic success team is important. Furthermore, individuals selected to oversee student athletes' academic progress need to be familiar with NCAA eligibility rules and the unique challenges facing those who are seeking to transfer to NCAA institutions following graduation from a community college.

Governing Entities. Institutions need to consider their participation and involvement in various governing entities, such as junior college athletic leagues and conferences, the NCAA, and the National Association of Intercollegiate Athletics (NAIA), when considering future expenses. Involvement with these associations, although voluntary, is recommended to ensure that athletic personnel support staff and faculty are adequately trained in NCAA and NAIA Eligibility Center requirements. This will ensure that student athletes are academically prepared and athletically eligible to matriculate to a four-year institution once they have exhausted their first two years of athletic eligibility. Additionally, there may be community college leagues and organizations with rules that must be adhered to for competition. Associated costs might include travel for personnel to attend NCAA rules training sessions and seminars or travel to league or association meetings to stay abreast of current developments.

NEW DIRECTIONS FOR COMMUNITY COLLEGES • DOI: 10.1002/cc

The "Underbelly." In considering extending or developing an athletic program, it is important to recognize the behavior of potential competitors. For example, it has been observed that some institutions put winning first, far ahead of student success. There is anecdotal evidence that suggests some institutions, in the desire to win, have recruited entire teams from international locations, only to have them all return to their home country when legally required (Ashburn, 2007; "Elliot" interview, 2008). Also stemming from a desire for competitive success is a lack of focus on academics. This is the underbelly of competition and thus an important consideration in developing an athletic program.

Discussion and Implications

In recent history, many athletes seeking to play NCAA sports have found themselves attending preparatory schools until their academic performance was deemed adequate for NCAA eligibility. However, recent rule changes by the NCAA allow students to count only one core academic course completed after their high school graduation toward the academic requirements needed to be eligible for NCAA Division I sports (Wolverton, 2007). Thus it is likely that more student athletes will seek out opportunities to participate in athletics at the community college as they prepare academically to enter a four-year institution. Community colleges should see this as an opportunity to expand their sport offerings and attract local students. Institutions not offering athletics programs may lose these students to community colleges in other locations where athletes can continue to pursue both their academic and athletic interests.

As institutions look to add, maintain, or eliminate their athletic programs, the process should be approached like any other major institutional change. The athletic program should be given every possible chance to contribute to the institution's mission. Transparency in decision making and significant time and effort in gathering pertinent information should be part of program operations. A unique characteristic of community college athletics, as opposed to some levels of NCAA athletics, is that the focus is on the participant and the personal and academic development of the athlete. Community college athletics programs will not become a revenue source for the college, but the benefits given to the participants, students, and local community are abundant. The director of athletics at one community college summed it up best when she said, "Everyone involved in community college athletics should buy into the fact that it is about the athletes and not the spectator" (Keenum interview, 2008). If community college leaders can keep the needs of the athletes at the forefront of decision making, the result will be an athletic program that truly supports the mission of the institution and enhances the educational experience for all involved.

References

Ashburn, E. "To Increase Enrollment, Community Colleges Add More Sports." *Chronicle of Higher Education*, July 6, 2007, p. 31.

Berson, J. S. "Student Perceptions of the Intercollegiate Athletic Program at a Community College." Paper presented at annual convention of National Association of Student Personnel, Mar. 1996. Atlanta, Georgia.

Castañeda, C., Katsinas, S. G., and Hardy, D. E. "The Importance of Intercollegiate Athletics at Rural-Serving Community Colleges: A Policy Brief by the Education Policy Center at the University of Alabama for the MidSouth Partnership for Rural Community Colleges." 2006. Retrieved Aug. 14, 2008, from http://www.ruralcommunity colleges.org/docs/MSPBRIEFATHLETICS.pdf.

Cohen, A. M., and Brawer, F. B. *The American Community College*. San Francisco: Jossey-Bass, 2008.

Commission on Athletics. "Commission on Athletics." (n.d.). Retrieved July 19, 2008, from http://www.coasports.org/about.asp.

Dowd, A. C., and Grant, J. L. "Equity and Efficiency of Community College Appropriations: The Role of Local Financing." *Review of Higher Education*, 2006, 29(2), 167–194.

Dowd, A. C., and Grant, J. L. "Equity Effects of Entrepreneurial Community College Revenues." *Community College Journal of Research and Practice*, 2007, 32, 231–244.

Duderstadt, J., *Intercollegiate Athletics and the American University: A President's Perspective*. Ann Arbor: University of Michigan Press, 2003.

Gleazer, E. J., Jr. *The Community College: Values, Vision & Vitality*. Washington, D.C.: American Association of Community and Junior Colleges, 1980.

Horton, D., Jr. "Comparative Study of the Persistence and Academic Success of Florida Community College Student-Athletes and Non-Athlete Students: 2004–2007." Ph.D. dissertation, University of Florida, 2009.

Levin, J. S. "The Revised Institution: The Community College Mission at the End of the Twentieth Century." *Community College Review*, 2000, 28(2), 1–25.

McLellan, B. "Calhoun Cuts Sports." *Decatur Daily*, May 2001, pp. A1, A10.

Mullin, C. M., and Honeyman, D. S. "The Funding of Community Colleges: A Typology of State Funding Formulas." *Community College Review*, 2007, 35(2), 113–127.

National Junior College Athletic Association (NJCAA). "NJCAA Participation Figures." NJCAA National Headquarters, Colorado Springs, Colorado, 2008.

National Junior College Athletic Association. "Welcome to the NJCAA." (n.d.). Retrieved May 16, 2008, from http://www.njcaa.org/index.cfm.

Nazarian, J. "'Front Porch' Deserves Care." *NCAA News*, Feb. 26, 2007.

Northwest Athletic Association of Community Colleges. "Northwest Athletic Association of Community Colleges." (n.d.). Retrieved May 16, 2008, from http://www.nwaacc.org/index.php.

Reapple, R., Peery, D., and Hohman, H. "Athletics in Community and Junior Colleges." In J. Frey (ed.), *The Governance of Intercollegiate Athletics*. West Point, N.Y.: Leisure Press, 1982.

Rishe, P. J. "A Reexamination of How Athletic Success Impacts Graduation Rates: Comparing Student-Athletes to All Other Undergraduates." *American Journal of Economics and Sociology*, 2003, 62(2), 407–427.

Sperber, M. *Beer and Circus: How Big-Time College Sports Is Crippling Undergraduate Education*. New York: Holt, 2000.

Williams, M. R., Byrd, L., and Pennington, K. "Intercollegiate Athletics at the Community College." *Community College Journal of Research and Practice,* 2008, 32, 453–461.

Williams, M. R., and Pennington, K. "Community College Presidents' Perceptions of Intercollegiate Athletics." *Community College Enterprise*, 2006, 12(2), 91–104.

Wolverton, B. "NCAA Ruling on Preparatory Schools Could Send More Athletes to Junior Colleges." *Chronicle of Higher Education*, May 11, 2007, p. A48.

HEATHER J. LAWRENCE *is an assistant professor of sport management at Ohio University, where she teaches courses in intercollegiate athletics, facility and event management, and diversity and sport.*

CHRISTOPHER M. MULLIN *is a postdoctoral fellow at the Illinois Education Research Council.*

DAVID HORTON, JR., *is an assistant professor in the Department of Counseling and Higher Education at Ohio University.*

NEW DIRECTIONS FOR COMMUNITY COLLEGES • DOI: 10.1002/cc

5

This chapter offers an overview of the impact of Title IX on athletics in two-year institutions.

Gender Equity in Two-Year Athletic Departments: Part I

Ellen J. Staurowsky

Although it may seem strange today, in the early 1970s the idea of women students receiving scholarship assistance on the basis of their athletic ability was not a common occurrence. Some postsecondary institutions were offering female athletes scholarships before the passage of Title IX in 1972, but others steadfastly held to a no-athletic-scholarship policy, abiding by a philosophical belief that athletic scholarships were part and parcel of a commercialized male athletic model that favored winning over education and opened the door for pressurized recruiting practices, academic fraud, and athlete exploitation (Wushanley, 2004).

In 1973, scarcely a year after Title IX was passed, female athletes from Broward Community College and Marymount College, along with their coaches and administrators, participated in a lawsuit that settled this question once and for all. At issue in the case was a policy banning athletic scholarships for female athletes that had been adopted by the leaders of the Association for Intercollegiate Athletics for Women (AIAW), the organization that served as the governing body for women's college sports at the time. The result was a policy modification that allowed member institutions to award scholarship assistance to women according to athletic ability. The case was significant because it went to the core of issues related to defining gender equity in athletic programs. In effect, resources available to male athletes could not be denied to female athletes as a constitutional matter under the Equal Protection clause of the Fourteenth Amendment and Title IX of the Education Amendments of 1964, regardless of intent (Wushanley, 2004).

NEW DIRECTIONS FOR COMMUNITY COLLEGES, no. 147, Fall 2009 © 2009 Wiley Periodicals, Inc.
Published online in Wiley InterScience (www.interscience.wiley.com) • DOI: 10.1002/cc.377

Despite the role that female athletes at the community college level played in this defining moment, it is interesting to note that there is little in the way of a comprehensive history of women's college sports at two-year institutions. To situate the current state of gender equity in athletic programs in two-year institutions in context, this chapter presents a brief historical overview of women in two-year athletic program leadership and then discusses how two-year athletic associations and commissions have defined gender equity, essential understandings of Title IX as applied to athletic programs, and the research that has been done on issues related to gender equity in athletic departments in two-year institutions.

Women in Two-Year Athletic Program Leadership

Caught between educationally based sport structures that have garnered more economic, political, and social capital over the years, and conceived of more as way stations than ultimate destinations by the public and participants alike, two-year athletic programs have not inspired the kind of research attention that has been directed toward four-year college and university programs. Even less attention has been directed toward the role of women leaders in two-year athletic programs. The scant information available does furnish an important anchor, however, for discussion of current gender equity in two-year athletic programs.

In one of the few histories of community college sports programs, Haugen (1990) traced the development of women's programs in community colleges in San Diego from 1955 to 1972. This work documents the resistance that women physical educators encountered from their own administration and from men's athletics faculties when they tried to establish viable athletic programs for female students. Haugen offers evidence that this group of female physical educators were called on to be persistent in the face of professional obstacles born out of societal prejudices toward women parti-cipating in sport and general perceptions of female inferiority.

With the passage of Title IX in 1972, the governance structure for women's sports programs at two-year institutions was subsumed into existing structures for men's athletics more quickly than occurred at four-year institutions (Carpenter and Acosta, 2005; Wushanley, 2004). As Beers (1997) reported, "The COA established statewide regulations for both men and women students and became the first post-secondary institution in the United States to bring together men's and women's athletic programs under one code book" (p. 108). Within six years of the passage of Title IX, the Northwest Athletic Association of Community Colleges (NWAACC) would also combine men's and women's sports under the same umbrella (NWAACC, n.d.).

Pursuing a slightly different path, the National Junior College Athletic Association (NJCAA) hosted invitational championships for women starting in 1974. According to Sykes (2002), the NJCAA took the bold step of creating a separate women's division shortly thereafter. In addition to meeting the needs of female athletes, another stated goal of the NJCAA Women's Division for the past four decades has been implementation of a plan to "identify, attract, and develop the leadership potential of women" within each NJCAA region (NJCAA, n.d.).

Despite that stated goal, an analysis of the gender breakdown of NJCAA athletic directors for the 2001–02 academic year revealed that 12.4 percent of NJCAA athletic directors (63 of 507) were female (Radlinski, 2003). Noting the nearly twenty-five-point gap between representation of female athletes in NJCAA athletic programs in 2001–02 (36 percent) and that of women in the role of athletic director, Radlinski concluded that "continuing structural barriers, institutional budgetary considerations, and the on-going limited representation of women in administration of athletics creates a need to establish an equal partnership with men in the leadership of the NJCAA" (p. 5).

Athletic Association and Commission Statements: Gender Equity and Title IX

Awareness of the necessity of complying with Title IX and other pertinent state and federal legislation barring sex discrimination in school-based programs is manifest in policy statements found in all the junior college athletic associations or commissions mentioned earlier in this article. In comparing these statements, one finds differences in approach apparent. Whereas the NJCAA's approach is expressed in a philosophical statement about gender equity, the American Indian Higher Education Consortium (AIHEC) Athletic Commission and the NWAAC refer more specifically to Title IX itself either in their policy manual or on their Website. In contrast, the California Community College Athletic Association (CCCAA) incorporates several definitions regarding gender equity and nondiscrimination throughout its constitution and bylaws, while also offering members and the general public information regarding Title IX on the CCCAA Website.

The NJCAA philosophical statement on gender equity appears as part of the NJCAA's purpose statement, following sections on the women's division and leadership roles of women in two-year college athletic programs (NJCAA, n.d.). Adopting language crafted initially by the NCAA Gender Equity Task Force in 1992 (Sweet, 2002) that has since been taken up by numerous conferences and institutions, the statement reads in part: "An athletic program can be considered equitable when the participants in both the men's and the women's programs would accept as fair and equitable the overall program of the other gender" (NJCAA, n.d.).

Within the CCCAA constitution and bylaws, references to gender equity appear in several places. The CCCAA operationalizes gender equity as a "commitment" to fostering "an environment in which equitable athletic opportunities, benefits, and resources are available to all students, in which every person is treated with respect and dignity" (p. 2). Having established a Gender Equity Committee in 1995 (Beers, 1997), which became a standing committee of the CCCAA Management Council in 2007, the committee is charged with "providing leadership in gender equity issues through the development of programs and services that benefit CCCAA members" (COA Constitution and Bylaws, p. x).

Specific guidance with regard to Title IX compliance is furnished by three of the four associations, in their own ways. The AIHEC Athletic Commission has a statement on Title IX compliance in its Athletic Competition Policies and Guidelines document (AIHEC, 2006). In turn, the NWAAC directs members to the Washington State Board of Community and Technical Colleges Website. A section on gender equity in athletics is designed to assist "those who have the responsibility to ensure that intercollegiate athletics are equitably provided." A similar resource in the form of a brochure that can be accessed online was prepared for the COA Gender Equity Committee by the Santa Clarita (California) Community College District.

Title IX: The Essentials

To interpret findings from studies assessing Title IX compliance in athletic programs, basic information regarding institutional obligations under the Title IX enforcement scheme serves as an important operational reference. Fundamentally, Title IX of the Education Amendment to the 1964 Civil Rights Act is the law that offers protection against sex discrimination for students participating in programs offered by educational institutions that receive federal financial support. In relevant part, the statute reads:

> No person in the United States shall, on the basis of sex, be excluded from participation in, be denied the benefits of or be subjected to discrimination under any education program or activity receiving Federal financial assistance [Title IX of the Education Amendments of 1972, 44 Fed. Reg. at 71413].

Emerging out of the civil rights and women's movements (Blumenthal, 2005; Durrant, 1992), Title IX "represents a national commitment to end discrimination and establish a mandate to bring the excluded into the mainstream" (CCCAA, n.d., section "Gender Equity . . ."). Although Title IX does not specifically mention athletics, Valerie Bonnette (2004), consultant and coauthor notes that the intent to address sex discrimination in athletics was well established by the time the statute came before the United States Congress in 1974. With a purpose of barring sex discrimination and fostering equitable opportunity and quality of treatment for female and male athletes, the law does not require cuts in men's programs to comply with Title IX (Kort 2008).

The requirements for Title IX compliance are clarified and outlined in the 1979 Intercollegiate Athletics Interpretation, otherwise known as the Policy Interpretation. It is in the Policy Interpretation where a measure of athletic participation opportunities known as the "three-part test" is found. Institutions may reach compliance by satisfying one of the three parts of the test:

1. Intercollegiate athletic participation opportunities for male and female students are provided in numbers substantially proportionate to their respective enrollments.
2. The institution can show a history of continuing practice of program expansion that is demonstrably responsive to the developing interests and abilities of the members of the underrepresented group of athletes.
3. The institution can demonstrate that the interests and abilities of the members of the underrepresented sex have been fully and effectively accommodated by the present program.

Substantial proportionality is determined by comparing the percentage of women athletes to the percentage of women within the overall student population. The closer the gap between these figures, the closer the program is to being substantially proportionate. A gap no larger than 3–5 percent is generally considered to be acceptable (Cohen, 2005).

The design of the compliance standards offers higher education administrators considerable latitude in developing compliance plans that best reflect the mission of their institution, the composition of their undergraduate full-time enrollment, and their economic circumstances. Ability to compete goes beyond equal access; "Title IX also includes a general requirement that schools treat men and women equally throughout their athletic programs" (Cohen, 2005). Although this requirement does not mean that male and female athletes must be treated exactly the same in every instance, program components that substantially affect the quality of the experience for athletes must be equivalent, including equipment and supplies, scheduling of games and practices, travel and per diem expenses, opportunities to receive coaching and academic assistance, locker rooms and facilities, athletic training services, housing and dining services, and publicity. Further, schools are also required to distribute athletic scholarship assistance equitably (Bonnette, 2004; Carpenter and Acosta, 2005; Cohen, 2005).

In 2004, the U.S. Supreme Court determined that coaches and administrators were protected under Title IX against retaliation from employers for seeking remedies to existing gender inequities in athletic programs (*Jackson v. Birmingham*, 2004).

As a matter of public information, schools receiving federal financial assistance are required to disclose resource allocations and rate of participation in their athletic programs, distributing the information to male and female athletes and teams through the yearly Equity in Athletics Disclosure Act (EADA) report form. Available by institution or in aggregate form, this information offers a mechanism for transparency to monitor efforts undertaken by institutions in meeting the mandate of Title IX (Carpenter and Acosta, 2005).

Gender Equity in Two-Year Athletic Programs

A decade after the passage of Title IX, Stier (1983) investigated the status of physical education and athletics programs in two-year institutions. When asked to respond to questions about Title IX, the administrators in the study offered contradictory perceptions. On the one hand, only 28 percent of the respondents felt Title IX had an effect on programs at their institutions, but by contrast 92 percent indicated their programs were in compliance. Although Stier could not offer a definitive reason for this discrepancy, he did speculate that the view shared by an administrator in the open comment section may have offered some insight into this apparent disconnect. The administrator wrote, "A department is in compliance until the government declares it is not in compliance" (p. 11).

Since the time of that early survey, a growing collection of studies focusing on Title IX compliance in two-year athletic programs has emerged. As a group, these studies reveal a trend consistently showing that female athletes are underrepresented compared to their representation in the student population overall. Whereas failure to meet the proportionality standard of the three-part test does not automatically imply that the majority of two-year institutions remain out of compliance with Title IX, analyses that explore factors beyond participation alone also reveal disproportionate allocations of financial resources and staffing.

In a study of Title IX compliance in athletic programs in California community colleges, Beers (1997) reported that participation opportunities for male and female athletes were not substantially proportionate to their relative enrollments. Although athletic directors believed that female athletes were being given opportunities commensurate with their interests and abilities, the majority expressed a belief that there were "serious problems with gender equity in California community colleges" (p. 44).

In a 2004 study of Title IX athletics compliance at California's public high schools, community colleges, and universities (Beam, Faddis, and Ruzicka, 2004), the greatest gender disparity identified in community colleges was in the area of participation. Of the ninety-one schools responding to the survey, only 8 percent reported a participation rate that was within five percentage points of enrollment for each gender. Additionally, 84 percent of those programs acknowledged participation percentages described in the report as "considerably outside the range of acceptability" (p. xi). More than half of the community colleges in the study reported relying on part two of the three-part test (having a history of continuing program expansion) as their chosen mode of achieving Title IX compliance.

Individual institutions may in fact be working toward the goal of incrementally expanding opportunities for female athletes. However, from a comparison of men's and women's sport participation conducted by the CCCAA Commission on Athletics in 2004, spanning the academic years 2000–01 through 2003–04, women's participation remained at 34–35 percent and the number of women participating actually declined from 7,537 to 7,348 over that span of time when enrollments were escalating. Beyond participation, Beam, Faddis, and Ruzicka (2004) also reported that men's teams averaged access to more head coaches and more FTEs compared to women's teams. Head coaches of men's teams had more experience than women's teams, and experience was correlated with higher salaries for coaches of men's teams.

The trends found in California community colleges signaling potential problems with Title IX compliance are not isolated ones. Examining the state of gender equity in community colleges in the state of Maryland, Mumford (1998, 2004) found that female athletes were not participating at a rate substantially proportional to enrollment and that opportunities available to female athletes to compete had declined during the period of time under investigation. Women made up 32 percent of the athlete population, but they accounted for 61 percent of the total enrollment in Maryland community colleges, resulting in a twenty-nine-point gap. Broadening his analysis to include examination of the gender representation among athletic directors, Mumford (2008) found that 89 percent of athletic directors were male.

The gender inequalities seen in Maryland community colleges were also found in two-year institutions in Pennsylvania (Cohen, 2005) and Ohio (Staurowsky with Morris, Paule, and Reese, 2007). Using a measure called an "athletic equity difference," which represents the proportionality gap between female athlete participation and female enrollment, NJCAA schools in Pennsylvania registered gaps of 19 and 20 percent for the 2001–02 and 2002–03 academic years respectively. In Ohio, gaps for NJCAA institutions ranged from 14.4 percent in 2003–04 to 16 percent in 2005–06, with a high of 25.99 percent during the 2004–05 academic year, according to Staurowsky and colleagues (2007).

In Cheslock's analysis (2007) of college athlete participation in two- and four-year institutions in relationship to program expansion and secondary school participation nationwide between 2000–01 and 2004–05, schools in neither the NJCAA nor the COA fared well in terms of proportionality, reporting gaps of 16.3 and 19.4 percent respectively. The NWAACC, though registering a 9.5 percent proportionality gap, exhibited a better record among two-year institutions, but that gap is nevertheless considered high in comparison to the recognized three-to-five-point gap expected for substantial proportionality to be achieved. Taking into account modest fluctuations in program offerings during the same time period, little evidence is available to support a conclusion that two-year institutions as a group were successful in achieving Title IX compliance by relying on a history of program expansion.

In perhaps the most comprehensive look at gender equity in community college athletic programs to date, Castañeda, Katsinas, and Hardy (2008) reported mixed results for Title IX compliance in accommodating student interest and ability. Whereas community colleges during the academic year 2002–03 offered nearly the same number of athletic teams for men as for women (565 to 558), the percentage of opportunities to compete heavily favored male athletes (63 percent of all athletes were male in that reporting year). A bright spot for female athletes was found in the area of athletically related financial aid, where 42 percent of all athletes receiving scholarship assistance were women, a figure that surpassed the representation of women in the overall athlete population.

Given the findings across these studies, it would seem difficult for institutions to continue to argue that they have plans in place to remedy gender inequities in participation and other areas of resource allocations in their athletic programs because of the modest gains of female athletes over the expanse of time covered. Further, female participation at the high school level continued to grow during this same period of time. As of this writing, according to the National Federation of State High School Associations (2008) female varsity athletes at the high school level number well over three million. The roughly 600,000 college and university athletes who compete in two- and four-year colleges and universities, approximately 210,000 of whom are women, would suggest that there are more female athletes with interest and ability than are currently being served by the present college sport system.

Past Is Prologue

As the second part of this chapter shows, Shakespeare's observation that what is past is prologue is very much in evidence when it comes to gender equity in two-year college athletic programs. There remains much work to be done in achieving a standard of gender equity that not only meets the intent of Title IX but also fully affords respect and dignity for female students and the athletic department personnel serving them.

References

American Indian Higher Education Consortium (AIHEC). "Athletic Competition Policies and Guidelines," 2006. Retrieved June 12, 2009, from http://www.aihec.org/colleges/documents/AthleticCompetitionGuidelines.pdf.
Beam, M., Faddis, B., and Ruzicka, P. "Title IX Athletics Compliance at California's Public High Schools, Community Colleges, and Universities." Prepared for California Postsecondary Education Commission and California Department of Education. RMC Research Consortium, Portland, Ore., 2004. Retrieved June 12, 2009, from http://www.women.ca.gov/index.php?option=com_content&view=article&id=120&Itemid=99.
Beers, S. A. "The Extent to Which California Community College Athletic Programs Are in Compliance with Title IX." Unpublished doctoral dissertation, Pepperdine University, 1997.
Blumenthal, J. Let Me Play: The Story of Title IX. The Law That Changed the Future of Girls in America. New York: Simon & Schuster, 2005.
Bonnette, V. Title IX and Intercollegiate Athletics: How It All Works—in Plain English. Self-published, 2007.

California Community College Athletic Association. "CCCAA Commission on Athletics Five-Year Comparison Men's and Women's Sport Participation," 2004. Retrieved June 12, 2009, from http://www.coasports.org/pdf/sport_comparison_5yr.pdf.

California Community College Athletic Association (CCCAA). *Constitution and Bylaws, 2008–2009.* (n.d.) Retrieved June 12, 2009, from http://www.coasports.org/constitution.asp.

Carpenter, L., and Acosta, V. *Title IX.* Champaign, Ill.: Human Kinetics, 2005.

Castañeda, C., Katsinas, S. G., and Hardy, D. E. "The Importance of Intercollegiate Athletics at Rural-Serving Community Colleges." 2005. Retrieved Nov. 22, 2008, from http://www.ruralcommunitycolleges.org/policy.htm.

Castañeda, C., Katsinas, S. G., and Hardy, D. E. "Meeting the Challenge of Gender Equity in Community College Athletics." In J. Lester (ed.), *Gendered Perspectives on Community College.* San Francisco: Jossey-Bass, 2008.

Cheslock, J. "Who's Playing College Sports? Trends in Participation, 2007." East Meadow, N.Y.: Women's Sports Foundation. Retrieved June 12, 2009, from http://www.womenssportsfoundation.org.

Cohen, D. "Gender Equity in Intercollegiate Athletics: Where Does Pennsylvania Stand?" 2005. Philadelphia: Women's Law Project. Retrieved Nov. 25, 2008, from http://www.womenslawproject.org.

Durrant, S. "Title IX: Its Power and Its Limitations." *Journal of Health, Physical Education, Recreation, and Dance,* Mar. 1992, 60–64.

Haugen, N. E. "A History of Women's Intercollegiate Athletics in San Diego Community Colleges from 1955 to 1972." Unpublished dissertation, University of San Diego, 1990.

Jackson v. Birmingham Board of Education (02–1672) 544 U.S. 167 (2005) 309 F.3d 1333.

Kort, M. "Full Court Press." *Ms.,* Spring 2008. Retrieved Nov. 28, 2008, from http://www.msmagazine.com/spring2008/fullCourtPress.asp.

Mumford, V. *Teams on Paper: Title IX Compliance in the Maryland Junior College Athletic Conference.* Unpublished doctoral dissertation, University of Delaware, 1998.

Mumford, V. "A Look at Women's Participation in Sports in Maryland Two-Year Colleges." *Sports Journal,* 2004, 8(1). Retrieved June 12, 2009, from http://www.thesportjournal.org/article/look-womens-participation-sports-maryland-two-year-colleges.

National Federation of State High School Associations. 2007–2008 High School Athletics Participation Survey, 2008. Retrieved July 17, 2009, from http://www.nfhs.org/core/contentmanager/uploads/2007-08%20Participation%20Survey.pdf.

National Junior College Athletic Association. "About NJCAA-Purpose Papers: Women's Division." (n.d.) Retrieved Nov. 5, 2008, from http://www.njcaa.org/purpose.cfm.

Northwest Athletic Association of Community Colleges. "NWAACC History and Growth." (n.d.) Retrieved Nov. 25, 2008, from http://www.nwaacc.org/history.php.

"Policy Interpretation: Title IX and Intercollegiate Athletics." *Federal Register,* Dec. 11, 1979, 44(239).

Radlinski, A. M. "Women in Athletic Administration in Community Colleges: Identification of Career Paths, Strategies and Competencies Found in Preparation for Leadership Roles in Athletics." Unpublished doctoral dissertation, Central Michigan University, 2003.

Staurowsky, E. J., with Morris, H., Paule, A., and Reese, J. "Travelers on the Title IX Compliance Highway: How Are Ohio's Colleges and Universities Faring?" *Women in Sport and Physical Activity Journal,* 2007, 15(40), 46–63.

Stier, W. "The Status of Physical Education Within Junior/Community Colleges." Paper presented at annual meeting of American Alliance for Health, Physical Education, Recreation, and Dance, Minneapolis, April, 1983.

Sweet, J. M. "Written Testimony of Judith M. Sweet, Senior Vice President, Championships and Education Services, National Collegiate Athletic Association." Presented before U.S. Secretary of Education's Commission on Opportunities in Athletics, Aug. 27, 2002. Retrieved Nov. 29, 2008, from http://www1.ncaa.org/membership/ed_outreach/gender_equity/resource_materials/upload/2002_sweet_testimony.htm.

Sykes, K. "Written Testimony of Karen Sykes, President, National Junior College Athletic Association." Presented before U.S. Secretary of Education's Commission on Opportunities in Athletics, Sept. 17, 2002.

Washington State Board for Community and Technical Colleges. "Self-Evaluation of Compliance with Title IX Regulations." Retrieved Nov. 25, 2008, from http://www.sbctc.ctc.edu/College/_s-selfevalenter.aspx.

Wushanley, Y. *Playing Nice and Losing: The Struggle for Control of Women's Intercollegiate Athletics 1960–1972.* Syracuse, N.Y.: Syracuse University Press, 2004.

ELLEN J. STAUROWSKY *is professor and graduate chair in the Department of Sport Management and Media at Ithaca College.*

NEW DIRECTIONS FOR COMMUNITY COLLEGES • DOI: 10.1002/cc

This chapter examines the current state of gender equity in athletic programs offered at two-year institutions.

Gender Equity in Two-Year College Athletic Departments: Part II

Ellen J. Staurowsky

In a series on college sport that appeared in the *New York Times* in the spring of 2007, the power of athletics to create a brand image for four-year colleges and universities was demonstrated in a slide show that displayed only the pompoms of seven mystery schools. The challenge for the reader so inclined was to identify the school on the basis of the colors alone. With that mere suggestion, the names of the nation's powerhouse athletic programs— Florida, Penn State, Notre Dame, Tennessee, North Carolina, Michigan, and Alabama—were evoked easily and, well, shall we say, with a bit of fanfare (Kahn, 2007).

In contrast, no such comparable fanfare accompanies discussion of athletic programs at two-year institutions. As writer Robert Andrew Powell (2007) pointed out, "Intercollegiate athletics at junior colleges . . . are largely anonymous, followed mostly by recruitniks and other talent obsessives" (n.p.). As resonant as that depiction of community college athletics is, it belies the complexity of the sensitive ecosystem within which athletic programs in two-year institutions exist and obscures the factors that shape two-year athletic programs across the nation.

Reflective of this unique status, Karen Sykes, president of the NJCAA, commented on the tenuous position that athletic programs occupy in two-year institutions in comparison to their secondary and four-year counterparts, in testimony before the U.S. Secretary of Education's Commission on Opportunities in Athletics in 2002:

NEW DIRECTIONS FOR COMMUNITY COLLEGES, no. 147, Fall 2009 © 2009 Wiley Periodicals, Inc.
Published online in Wiley InterScience (www.interscience.wiley.com) • DOI: 10.1002/cc.378

Two-year athletics offer up somewhat of a black hole, recognized by some, totally ignored by others. Called upon at times to support broad based issues of shared importance and criticized at others, we represent a large constituency that doesn't fit neatly with either secondary schools or four-year colleges.

Historically, funding for two-year institutions has come from a combination of federal, state, and local government sources, private gifts, and grants, as well as student tuition. Chronic budget deficits affecting higher education spending in many states in recent years had already raised concerns about the immediate short- and long-term future and stability of state investments in higher education (Katsinas, Palmer, and Tollefson, 2004). In 2008, the nation's mortgage crisis, the failure of the financial markets, rising unemployment, diminishing access to student loans, and widening fiscal crises in state governments contributed significantly to weakening an already insecure financial base for two-year institutions (Busby, 2008; Pugh, 2008; Selingo, 2008).

A sign of the trouble that lies ahead is found in a survey of members of the National Council of State Directors of Community Colleges released in 2008. According to that survey, eighteen of twenty-eight states with community college funding formulas failed to fully finance them in 2007–08, and community colleges were subjected to the largest one-year drop in state appropriations between 2006–07 and 2007–08 of any sector of public education (Pugh, 2008).

As a part of two-year institutions, athletic programs are not immune to the systemic fiscal realities and vulnerabilities confronting community college administrators that affect the entire enterprise. In a case study examining the perceptions of a group of ten community college presidents regarding intercollegiate athletics, financing was described as a "never ending" concern (Burgess, 2006). Gauging the fiscal health of two-year athletic programs is at best problematic given the variability in models used in funding athletic programs, which rely on some combination of state support where permitted, booster organizations, student fees, and external revenue streams. As a result, the precautionary note sounded by the *Community College Review* ("Athletics in Community Colleges," n.d.) that few generalizations can be made about community college athletics programs seems reasonable.

This diversity in scope, scale, and purpose among two-year college athletic programs, considered in light of turbulent economic times, was a necessary backdrop against which discussion regarding gender equity in athletic programs can be framed. At the same time, the fact that 60 percent of all students attending two-year institutions are women similarly requires ongoing attention (American Association of Community Colleges, 2008).

Two overarching questions have guided the research done for this article. First, how successful have two-year institutions been in responding to the mandate of Title IX of the Education Amendments Act of 1964? Second, as decision makers at two-year institutions devise strategies to weather difficult economic circumstances, how will the principles of gender equity be preserved when revisiting planning priorities for athletics?

The remainder of this chapter addresses these guiding questions through:

- A brief overview of athletics and funding in two-year institutions
- Analysis of participation and resource allocations for a four-year time period between 2004–05 and 2006–07, based on Equity in Athletics Disclosure Report data
- A summary of four cases that emerged in 2008 alleging Title IX violations in two-year athletic programs

The chapter concludes with consideration of challenges and opportunities that lie ahead in achieving gender equity in athletic departments in two-year institutions.

A Brief Overview of Athletics and Funding in Two-Year Institutions

Nearly half of all two-year institutions offer intercollegiate athletic programs, which are as widely diverse as their home institutions ("Athletics in Community Colleges," n.d.). Reflective of this diversity, four sport governing associations offer championships for community and tribal college participants: the American Indian Higher Education Consortium Athletic Commission (37 member institutions representing approximately 1,000 athletes), the California Community College Athletic Association (CCCAA) Commission on Athletics (143 member schools representing 25,000 athletes), the National Junior College Athletic Association (NJCAA; 530 institutions and 50,000 athletes), and the Northwest Athletic Association of Community Colleges (NWAACC; 36 member institutions and 3,614 athletes).

According to Bryd and Williams (2007), the development of athletic programs within community colleges has been sporadic and haphazard. Some states such as Alaska and Hawaii have determined athletics to be too cost-prohibitive, but nearly all of the community colleges in California sponsor intercollegiate athletics programs (Castañeda, Katsinas, and Hardy, 2005).

Lack of research regarding the role of athletic programs within community colleges creates information gaps for higher education decision makers. Whereas some community college leaders are turning to sport as a way of increasing enrollment by appealing to the interests of local as well as out-of-state or out-of-region students, it remains to be determined if the student benefits, public recognition, community goodwill, and economic impact thought to accrue from athletic programs justify the investments made by these schools. As Williams, Byrd, and Pennington (2008) point out:

At the community college level, it is unclear whether growth in the number and scope of programs is thoughtfully planned or occurring without benefit of discussions on how new teams are established, whether the institutional budget supports athletics, and whether intercollegiate athletics support the mission and philosophy of the college [n.p.].

According to a recent study by Williams and Pennington (2006), 79 percent of the community college presidents who responded did not believe athletics had a secure funding base, while 64 percent did not believe that budgets for athletics are well understood. If the vast majority of community college athletic programs rely on insecure funding models, where does that leave discussion regarding gender equity and program development for women athletes?

An Analysis of Gender Equity in Two-Year Athletic Programs

As a means of analyzing trends in the opportunities available and support devoted to women's athletics in community college programs, an analysis of EADA data was conducted for a four-year span of time between the academic years of 2003–04 through 2006–07 (all data for this section is on file with the author). The dataset included 555 public two-year institutions because this was the most comprehensive set of data available. Gender breakdowns for the five reporting areas were analyzed over this time period: (1) student enrollment, (2) athletic participation, (3) athletically related student aid, (4) recruiting expenses, and (5) operating expenses.

To understand the analysis to follow, the Title IX basics covered in Chapter Five are helpful. As discussed there, the Title IX three-part test directs schools to achieve compliance in the area of athletic participation through one of three ways:

- The proportionality standard (where the percentage of female athletes reflects the percentage of females in the student body)
- Through a history and continuing practice of program expansion (meaning that a school may not be offering proportional opportunities to female athletes but the school has consistently sought to expand opportunities, by adding teams for instance)
- Through accommodating the interest and abilities of female athletes

Based on the EADA data for the time period between 2003–04 and 2006–07, women made up 55 percent of the overall student population. Compared to the gender breakdown in athletic participation, an inverse representation existed, where 63 percent of all athletes were male and 37 percent female. The proportion of female athletes (55 percent) compared to the proportion of female students (37 percent) showed an athletic equity difference or gap of 18 percent.

NEW DIRECTIONS FOR COMMUNITY COLLEGES • DOI: 10.1002/cc

Although Title IX compliance must be done case by case, when this finding is considered in light of previous research it is clear that two-year athletic programs are not generally offering athletic opportunities to female students substantially proportionate to their enrollment (Beers, 1997; Beam, Faddis, and Ruzicka 2004; Castañeda, Katsinas, and Hardy, 2005; Cheslock, 2007, Cohen, 2005; Mumford, 2004, 2006, Staurowsky, with Morris, Paule, and Reese, 2007). Previous research established that proportionality gaps from the mid-1990s through 2003 were 16–29 percent depending on the sector under investigation. The 18 percent athletic equity difference would suggest that provision of opportunities for female athletes within two-year athletic programs is in a holding pattern. Such a holding pattern would argue against claims that two-year athletic programs were attempting to satisfy Title IX requirements by addressing the second part of the three-part test (demonstrating a history and continuing practice of program expansion); see Chapter Five of this volume for a more detailed explanation of the three-part test.

What further complicates this picture is the decline in actual numbers of both male and female athletes during this window of time. Between 2003–04 and 2006–07, the number of male athletes declined by 188 while the number of female athletes declined by 493. Although it is difficult to discern what may account for these declines, the fact that it was greater for female athletes has implications for how effectively an institution could argue that it is addressing any aspect of the three-part test.

Taken in the aggregate, the reporting institutions appear to be complying with Title IX fairly well in the area of athletically related aid. Whereas the standard of compliance in this area is for schools to award financial aid to female athletes within a percentage point of their representation within the athlete population, schools seem to be awarding more scholarship assistance to female athletes than required under Title IX. Whereas 37 percent of athletes are female, they are receiving 44 percent of the athletically related scholarship assistance. That being said, proportional allocation of financial assistance on the basis of female athletic participation should not be misconstrued. In the end, female athletes in the community college setting had access to roughly $6–7 million less in financial assistance than male athletes.

Allocation of resources in the area of recruiting disproportionately favored men's programs 59 percent to 41 percent over all four years. Whereas operating expenditures also favor men's programs, there is greater fluctuation in this area from year to year; women's share of the budget improved from 35 percent in academic year 2003–04 to 39 percent in 2006–07.

Whereas the EADA data highlight what are likely to be areas of inequity within two-year athletic programs, and administrators may wish to address shortfalls, recent Title IX complaints at two-year institutions illustrate how these vulnerabilities may play out on individual campuses.

New Directions for Community Colleges • DOI: 10.1002/cc

Pending Title IX Cases and Complaints at Two-Year Institutions

In an article published in 2006 in the *Community College Journal of Research and Practice*, researcher Vincent Mumford observed: "Although lawsuits for gender discrimination in intercollegiate athletics are nearly unheard of at the 2-year college level, administrators should consider themselves lucky. Nearly all 2-year colleges are vulnerable to Title IX lawsuits" (p. 220). The year 2008 may well signal the fact that luck has run out for two-year colleges with regard to flying below the radar screen on issues pertaining to Title IX compliance and gender equity in athletic programs. To date, there are at least four cases that could potentially have a serious affect on future compliance: Cabrillo College (Steeg, 2008); *Sulpizio and Bass* v. *San Diego Mesa Community College* (2008); *Wartluft* v. *Feather River Community College* (AAUW, 2008); and a Title IX complaint filed against Weatherford College in Texas ("Weatherford College . . . ," 2008).

In *Wartluft*, the key facts in the case center on whether former head coach and faculty member Laurel Wartluft was retaliated against for complaining of sex discrimination in violation of Title IX (AAUW, 2008). As of this writing, the case is scheduled to go to trial in May 2010 (AAUW, 2009).

The athletic department at San Diego Mesa Community College has been the subject of both a Title IX investigation by the U.S. Department of Education Office for Civil Rights (OCR) and a lawsuit filed by two former female coaches. In September 2008, the Department of Education issued a finding that San Diego Mesa was in violation of Title IX, describing the disparities found to be "substantial and unjustified" and "more than negligible" ("Department of Education . . . ," 2008; Associated Press, 2008). According to the OCR, disparities were found in the college's scheduling of games, use of locker rooms, use of practice and competitive facilities, and provisions for medical and training support (Associated Press, 2008).

The U.S. Department of Education's investigation of San Diego Mesa was the result of a complaint filed by former head women's basketball coach Lorri Sulpizio and her domestic partner, former director of basketball operations Kathy Bass. The finding in the investigation occurred after their termination from San Diego Mesa. In the pending lawsuit they have filed against San Diego Mesa and its agents, Sulpizio and Bass allege that they were retaliated against for speaking out about gender inequities, were subject to gender and sexual orientation discrimination, and were wrongly dismissed in violation of public policy (*Sulpizio and Bass* v. *San Diego Mesa College*, 2008).

Similar to the Feather River and Mesa cases, which involve alleged institutional retaliation against employees advocating for gender equity, Weatherford College (WC) was sued in May 2009 by one-time athletic director and current women's basketball coach Bob McKinley (Scott, 2009). This suit follows a complaint filed with the U.S. Department of Education Office for Civil Rights (OCR) in 2008 that raised questions regarding access, opportunity, and resources ("WC Answers . . . ," 2008; "Weatherford College . . . ," 2008).

According to Weatherford's EADA filing for the 2007–08 academic year, female athletes were underrepresented in proportion to female enrollment by 27 percent and male athletes in that year had access to nearly twice the athletic opportunities available to female athletes (Bassham, 2008). This gap by itself is not evidence of a Title IX violation by itself, but it may explain why the OCR initiated the inquiry. Other potential areas of concern, according to the available EADA data, center on athletically related student aid, where men's teams were allocated $236,370 and women's teams were allocated $143,166; and operating revenues, where men's teams were allocated $580,696 compared to $390,132 for women's teams (Bassham, 2008).

The institutional history in this case is complicated, however. From accounts dating back to 2003, administrators at Weatherford were aware that the institution was not in compliance with Title IX. At that time, the WC board of trustees was engaged in a process to review the start-up and operational costs to add a second scholarship sport for women. The board tabled the agenda item, directing administrators to prepare a more detailed actual-cost-versus-revenue report on the entire athletic department ("Board Discusses . . . ," 2003). The review process resulted in the hiring, in the summer of 2008, of a full-time athletic director who was charged with the task of developing a Title IX plan to address the existing inequities in the program.

In spring 2009, the OCR did find the institution in violation of Title IX but was willing to terminate the investigation on the basis of the college's commitment to take action. That said, the agreement reached between the OCR and WC was reported to give the institution time to survey the interests of female athletes to determine if their needs were being met, raising doubts as to whether anything would change on the WC campus ("WC Gender Equity . . . ," 2009). In an interesting twist, however, four concerned citizens ran for election to the Weatherford board of trustees on the "Right Choice for WC" ticket and eventually won seats on the board. They shared a platform that included a call for the college to treat female athletes equitably. During the first meeting of the new board in June 2009, an informal agreement was reached that the college would start a softball team in 2011 (Kennedy, 2009).

These cases reveal that Title IX compliance in athletic departments is being monitored at the community college level and institutions may be vulnerable to complaints and lawsuits. The cost of such litigation can be extremely high, not only in time and effort to respond to complaints but in the cost of litigation itself. In the state of California, awards and settlements in what have come to be called the *Fresno* cases (all involving female coaches and administrators at the California State University at Fresno who won major financial compensation amounting to millions of dollars for the sex-discriminatory and retaliatory manner in which they were treated as a result of advocating for gender equity) resulted in a statewide commission to monitor Title IX compliance in schools (Kort, 2008).

At the time of passage of Title IX in 1972, the vast majority of educational institutions in the United States could rely on a stipulation in the enforcement guidelines that offered opportunities for schools to create and implement Title IX compliance plans in athletic departments (Carpenter and Acosta, 2005). In effect, schools were afforded time to consider funding issues, develop staffing plans, and resolve facilities issues needed to fully and effectively accommodate female athletes. As the fourth decade since passage of Title IX approaches, persuasively arguing that school officials need more time to bring programs into compliance will be more difficult. This wave of recent cases suggests that proactive approaches to Title IX compliance may best serve institutions in the long run.

Considerations for the Future

Following their analysis of gender equity in community college athletic programs, Castañeda, Katsinas, and Hardy (2008) urged administrators to consider adding women's programs in cost-effective ways such as forging partnerships with local facilities to make the addition of programs more feasible, exploring plans to offer new women's programs in concert with local conferences to ensure reasonably accessible competition, and expanding both men's and women's programs in response to the interests and needs of female and male students. As worthy as those recommendations are, they were made before the subprime mortgage lending crisis, the rescue of automakers by the U.S. Congress, and the taxpayer bailout of the financial markets.

As higher education administrators rise to the challenge of an uncertain economic present, discussions regarding gender equity in athletic programs pale in comparison to the struggles of everyday Americans to keep a roof overhead, food on the table, gas in the car, and a job to go to each day. If there is any certainty to be found, it is in the assurance that, along with all other sectors of the higher education landscape, athletic programs are already shouldering the burden of financial cutbacks, and will continue to do so, while maintaining the heart and soul of the educational enterprise.

As institutional decision makers revisit programmatic and curricular priorities, the implications of cutting women's athletic programs should be thoroughly examined before those decisions are implemented. Program reductions that may appear to be equal on the surface, such as cutting back an equivalent number of athletic opportunities or contests for men and women, may in fact exacerbate an already imbalanced situation. As the research findings cited earlier show, the gender equity profile for two-year institutions in aggregate form indicates a strong likelihood that there are systemic inequities favoring male athletes. Where women's programs are already underfunded and female athletes are underrepresented within athletic departments, seemingly equal reductions in men's and women's programs have a greater negative impact on women's programs.

Further, the essence of a crisis is opportunity, and two-year institutions have a chance now to programmatically put the principle of gender equity at the center of discussions regarding restructuring athletic programs. To do so would require rethinking stereotypical attitudes regarding women's athletic participation. In a recent lecture at Smith College, economist Andrew Zimbalist noted that opposition to Title IX enforcement stems from claims that women are not as interested in participating in athletics as men (Choi, 2008). Citing the thirty-year record of growth in girls' and women's athletic participation since the passage of Title IX, Zimbalist argued, as have Cheslock (2007) and others as well, that the creation of opportunity drives interest. This mind-set has the potential to enable decision makers to see areas of development not previously considered that will ensure greater Title IX compliance and reduction in the vulnerabilities that community colleges face in terms of gender equity and intercollegiate athletics (Mumford, 2006). A new way of thinking about varsity athletics may well reflect the diversity of female students who attend two-year institutions, with provisions made accordingly.

This would require reassessment of attitudes regarding women athletes and rethinking the level of respect afforded to nontraditional women students who may wish to compete. A revealing exchange in the *New York Times* illustrates the point. Discussing the challenges of fielding women's teams, an athletic director at a community college in California remarked, "People say, 'How come our teams are always old women? I tell them it's because old women are the only ones we can find to play. Few high schools in the area are feeding us younger players" (Powell, 2007). In a year when mothers such as forty-one-year-old Dara Torres were celebrated for their successes at the 2008 Olympic Games, it is well worth considering reconceptualizing how athletic programs serve nontraditional-aged female students.

Finally, as two-year athletic programs consider new directions, fulfilling the promise of creating a greater voice for women leaders should also be considered. Allegations of retaliation against women coaches who have advocated on behalf of female athletes suggests that oppressive forces hampering the achievement of gender equity within two-year athletic programs still need to be addressed.

References

American Association of Community Colleges. "Community College Research and Statistics," 2008. Retrieved Nov. 22, 2008, from http://www2.aacc.nche.edu/research/index.htm.

American Association of University Women. *Wartluft v. Feather River Community College,* Sept. 2008. Retrieved Oct. 24, 2008, from http://www.aauw.org/advocacy/laf/cases/LW.cfm.

American Association of University Women. *Warluft v. Feather River Community College,* 2009. Retrieved July 17, 2009, from http://aauw.org/advocacy/laf/cases/LW.cfm.

American Indian Higher Education Consortium. "AIHEC Athletic Competition Policies and Guidelines," Mar. 2006. Retrieved June 18, 2009, from http://www.aihec.org /colleges/documents/AthleticCompetitionGuidelines.pdf.

Associated Press. "SD College Gets Mixed Review in Title IX Complaint." *Mercury News,* Sept. 16, 2008. Retrieved Nov. 28, 2008, from http://www.mercurynews.com/.

"Athletics in Community Colleges." *Community College Review,* n.d. Retrieved Nov. 24, 2008, from http://www.communitycollegereview.com/articles/10.

Bassham, K. "Equity in Athletic Disclosure Act Report: Weatherford College." 2008. Retrieved Nov. 28, 2008, from http://ope.ed.gov/athletics/.

Beam, M., Faddis, B., and Ruzicka, P. "Title IX Athletics Compliance at California's Public High Schools, Community Colleges, and Universities." Prepared for California Postsecondary Education Commission and California Department of Education. RMC Research Consortium, Portland, Ore., 2004. Retrieved June 12, 2009, from http://www.women.ca.gov/index.php?option=com_content&view=article&id=120&Itemid=99.

Beers, S. A. "The Extent to Which California Community College Athletic Programs Are in Compliance with Title IX." Unpublished doctoral dissertation, Pepperdine University, 1997.

"Board Discusses Title IX Compliance." Press release, Weatherford College, July 23, 2003, Weatherford, Tex. Retrieved Nov. 28, 2008, from http://www.wc.edu.

Burgess, C. D., "Perceptions of Selected Community College Presidents Regarding Certain Aspects of Intercollegiate Athletics," January 1, 2006. *ETD Collection for University of Nebraska-Lincoln.* Paper AAI3215459. Retrieved July 17, 2009, from http://digitalcommons.unl.edu/dissertations/AAI3215459.

Busby, R. "Two-Year Colleges Brace for Proration." *Alabama Press-Register,* Nov. 17, 2008. Retrieved Nov. 26, 2008, from http://www.al.com.

Byrd, L., and Williams, M. R. "Expansion of Community College Athletic Programs." *Community College Enterprise,* Fall 2007. Retrieved Nov. 24, 2008, from http//www.findarticles.com.

Carpenter, L., and Acosta, V. *Title IX.* Champaign, Ill.: Human Kinetics, 2005.

Castañeda, C., Katsinas, S. G., and Hardy, D. E. *The Importance of Intercollegiate Athletics at Rural-Serving Community Colleges.* Meridian, Miss.: Mid-South Partnership for Rural Community Colleges, 2005. Retrieved Nov. 22, 2008, from http://www.rural communitycolleges.org/policy.htm.

Castañeda, C., Katsinas, S. G., and Hardy, D. E. "Meeting the Challenge of Gender Equity in Community College Athletics." In J. Lester (ed.), *Gendered Perspectives on Community College.* San Francisco: Jossey-Bass, 2008.

Cheslock, J. "Who's Playing College Sports? Trends in Participation, June 2007." Women's Sports Foundation, East Meadow, N.Y. Retrieved June 18, 2009, from http://www.womenssportsfoundation.org.

Choi, J. "Smith Professor Speaks on Title IX." *Sophian,* 2008. Retrieved Dec. 4, 2008, from http://www.smithsophian.com/.

Cohen, D. "Gender Equity in Intercollegiate Athletics: Where Does Pennsylvania Stand?" Women's Law Project, Nov. 2005, Philadelphia. Retrieved Nov. 25, 2008, from http://www.womenslawproject.org.

"Department of Education, Office of Civil Rights Confirms Title IX Violations Alleged in Lawsuit." Press release, Sept. 17, 2008. Retrieved Nov. 28, 2008, from http://www.nclrights.org.

Kahn, J. "Color Combos: Can You Name the School?" *New York Times,* Jan. 7, 2007. Retrieved Nov. 22, 2008, from http://www.nytimes.com/indexes/2007/01/07/education/edlife/index.html.

Katsinas, S. G., Palmer, J. C., and Tollefson, T. A. "State Funding for Community Colleges: Perceptions from the Field. A Survey of the Members of the National Council of State Directors of Community Colleges." Oct. 26, 2004. Retrieved June 18, 2009, from http://www.coe.ilstu.edu/eafdept/centerforedpolicy/downloads/commcolleges-tudy.pdf.

Kennedy, B. "Weatherford College Trustees Plan New Playing Field by Adding Softball." *Dallas Star-Telegram*, June 18, 2009. Retrieved June 18, 2009, from http://www.star-telegram.com.

Kort, M. "Full Court Press." *Ms.*, 2008. Retrieved Nov. 28, 2008, from http://www.msmagazine.com.

Mumford, V. "A Look at Women's Participation in Sports in Maryland Two-Year Colleges," *Sports Journal*, 2005. Retrieved June 12, 2009, from http://www.thesportjournal.org/article/look-womens-participation-sports-maryland-two-year-colleges.

Mumford, V. "Promoting Equity and Access in 2-Year College Intercollegiate Athletic Programs." *Community College Journal of Research and Practice*, 2006, *30*, 213–222.

Powell, R. A. "Community College: Tennis in a Parking Lot." *New York Times*, Apr. 22, 2007. Retrieved Nov. 22, 2008, from http://www.nytimes.com/2007/04/22/education/edlife/sport22.html.

Pugh, T. "Economic Crisis Squeezing Colleges, Universities." McClatchy Washington Bureau, Nov. 19, 2008. Retrieved Nov. 26, 2008, from http://www.mcclatchydc.com/homepage/v-rint/story/56167.html.

Scott, G. "Coach Sues College." *Weatherford Democrat*, June 5, 2009. Retrieved June 18, 2009, from http://www.weatherforddemocrat.com.

Selingo, J. J. "State Budgets Are Likely to Squeeze 2-year Colleges." *California State University Northridge News Clippings*, Nov. 3, 2008. Retrieved Nov. 26, 2008, from http://www.blogs.csun.edu/news/.

Staurowsky, E. J., with Morris, H., Paule, A., and Reese, J. "Travelers on the Title IX Compliance Highway: How Are Ohio's Colleges and Universities Faring?" *Women in Sport and Physical Activity Journal*, 2007, *15*(40), 46–63.

Steeg, J. L. "Lawsuits, Disputes Reflect Continuing Tension over Title IX." *USA Today*, May 13, 2008. Retrieved Nov. 25, 2008, from http://www.usatoday.com.

Sulpizio and Bass v. *San Diego Mesa Community College* (July 24, 2008). Case no. 37–2008–00088329-CU-CR-CTL. Retrieved Nov. 28, 2008, from http://www.nclrights.org/site/PageServer?pagename=issue_sports.

Sykes, K. "Written Testimony of Karen Sykes, President, National Junior College Athletic Association." Presented before U.S. Secretary of Education's Commission on Opportunities in Athletics, Sept. 17, 2002.

"WC Answers Title IX Inquiry." Press release, Dec. 1, 2008. Weatherford, Tex.: Weatherford College. Retrieved Dec. 1, 2008, from http://wc.edu.

"WC Gender Equity Investigation Terminated." *Weatherford Democrat*, Mar. 11, 2009. Retrieved June 18, 2009, from http://www.weatherforddemocrat.com.

"Weatherford College Answers Title IX Inquiry." *Weatherford Democrat*, Nov. 28, 2008. Retrieved Nov. 28, 2008, from htpp://www.weatherforddemocrat.com.

Williams, M. R., Byrd, L., and Pennington, K. "Intercollegiate Athletics at the Community College." *Community College Journal of Research and Practice*, 2008, *32*, 453–461.

Williams, M. R., and Pennington, K. "Community College Presidents' Perceptions of Intercollegiate Athletics." *Community College Enterprise*, 2006. Retrieved Nov. 24, 2008, from http://www.findarticles.com.

ELLEN J. STAUROWSKY is professor and graduate chair in the Department of Sport Management and Media at Ithaca College.

NEW DIRECTIONS FOR COMMUNITY COLLEGES • DOI: 10.1002/cc

7

This chapter focuses on how student services support community college student athletes. Included are policy recommendations to help institutions develop programs to facilitate community college student athletes' current and future academic success.

Student Services and Student Athletes in Community Colleges

Jason Storch, Matthew Ohlson

From admissions to academic counseling, athletes will benefit from intense integration of support services and life-skills development programs to help balance the demands of their academic responsibilities and participation in athletics. Additionally, student support services at community colleges, even though attempting to assist students to graduate, must also be aware of the numerous four-year transfer issues that have an impact on student athletes' athletic eligibility. In addressing the needs of a diverse clientele, student services must focus on both retention of student athletes as well as recruitment of some athletes by four-year institutions.

In this chapter we discuss the student services that are essential to equip student athletes with the skills needed to achieve current and future goals. There is a glaring void in the available research focusing directly on the services afforded to student athletes in community and junior college settings. Our recommendations offer practitioners an abundance of strategies. These strategies have been used in one of the nation's most successful athletic programs. Though based on a four-year model, the recommendations include many of the same components required of an effective student support program for student athletes at two-year institutions of higher education.

The Need for Student Services

Higher education faculties often perceive student athletes as lacking the educational skills needed to succeed academically (Hobneck, Mudge, and Turchi, 2003). Yet when compared to their nonathlete counterparts, graduation and

NEW DIRECTIONS FOR COMMUNITY COLLEGES, no. 147, Fall 2009 © 2009 Wiley Periodicals, Inc.
Published online in Wiley InterScience (www.interscience.wiley.com) • DOI: 10.1002/cc.379

academic success rates actually favor student athletes (Gaston-Gayles, 2004; Umbach, Palmer, Kuh, and Hannah, 2006). One of the leading factors of the academic success of today's student athlete at both two- and four-year institutions is the presence of a strong student services program, which includes learning experiences and strategies leading to new skills, interests, work habits, and personal beliefs (Gaston-Gayles, 2004; Shurts and Shoffner, 2004). Strong student services programs ultimately lead to improved interpersonal skills and serve as a foundation for current and future success.

Making up more than 40 percent of all institutions of higher education, community colleges remain instrumental "avenues of opportunity" for more than ten million students annually (Mumford, 2006). Moreover, NCAA policy changes in 2008 have resulted in an increase in the number and types of coursework required for incoming prospective freshman student athletes to matriculate to four-year institutions. These NCAA policy changes are influencing four-year institutional eligibility for prospective student athletes and will likely result in continued growth in the enrollment of collegiate student athletes at the community college level. With a predicted rise in enrollment, the need for strong support services at the community college level, especially for those students from low socioeconomic (SES) background, will continue to grow (Ashburn, 2007; Knapp and Raney, 1988). This responsibility is then placed on the student advisement staff at the community college level to meet the diverse needs of the student athletes.

One of the most effective practices for the recruitment and retention of student athletes is a strong student support system. Services provided by community colleges often surpass those offered by four-year institutions (Keim and Strickland, 2004). Thanks to their greater institutional access and proclivity for enhanced faculty-student interactions, community colleges have increased recruitment and remedial services for underprepared students.

Community colleges have the opportunity to serve as models for better serving, supporting, and guiding all students, but in particular providing appropriate services for student athletes. Student athletes at community colleges are often motivated to succeed both athletically and academically in hopes of transferring to four-year institutions; however, without a strong student services program, these student athletes are less likely to graduate (Jenkins, 2006). Historically, components of effective student services programs have included eligibility monitoring, academic advising, academic testing, tutorial assistance, personal and career counseling, and mentoring (Gunn and Eddy, 1989; Lenz and Shy, 2003). In concert, Carodine, Almond, and Gratto (2001) state that the ideal program should include academic advising, life-skills development, and personal and professional counseling. This chapter offers a detailed examination of these three components plus specific recommendations from research and current community college and four-year institutional practices.

NEW DIRECTIONS FOR COMMUNITY COLLEGES • DOI: 10.1002/cc

Life-Skills Development. It has been argued that institutions of higher education have an obligation to help prepare student athletes for their future (Carodine, Almond, and Gratto, 2001). Student athletes may be less prepared and less independent than their nonathlete counterparts owing to regimented schedules. They may also have less time to devote to career development and career planning (Carodine, Almond, and Gratto, 2001; Kornspan and Etzel, 2001; Shurts and Shoffner, 2004). The participation of student athletes within a life-skills and career development program may help these students enhance student independence and maturity and guide them for their current and future success (Shurts and Shoffner, 2004; Kornspan and Etzel, 2001). An exemplary life-skills program may include these activities in a community college setting:

- Promote student athletes' ownership of their academic, athletic, career, personal, and community responsibilities.
- Meet the changing needs of student athletes.
- Promote respect for diversity and inclusion.
- Assist student athletes in identifying and applying transferable skills.
- Heighten awareness and education for the transfer to four-year institutions.
- Foster an environment that encourages student athletes to effectively access campus resources.
- Encourage development of character, integrity, and leadership skills.

The need for a comprehensive life-skills development program may be most important in the latter stages of a student's education. As a student athlete approaches the end of his or her athletic career, a shift occurs from emphasis placed on a career in athletics toward career options apart from sports (Lally and Kerr, 2005). Ultimately, the final outcome of a life-skills development program is twofold. First, a successful program will provide the tools and support for student athletes to transfer skills from the athletic field such as dedication, commitment, and teamwork to academic and professional skill sets. Additionally, it is the goal of a successful life-skills program to help the student athlete develop the skills, strategies, and efficacy necessary to address future challenges without the support of a counselor or advisor (Kornspan and Etzel, 2001; Shurts and Shoffner, 2004).

Exemplary programs also encourage student exposure and involvement in areas and activities that may bring greater career and life satisfaction (Shurts and Shoffner, 2004). As an exemplary program we offer the University of Florida's Collegiate Achievement Mentoring Program or C.A.M.P Gator. In this program, student athletes complete a comprehensive leadership-training curriculum and in turn serve as leadership mentors to at-risk middle-school children in the community. The hallmark of this program is an opportunity for student athletes to make a difference in the community while further enhancing their own leadership, goal setting, and public speaking abilities.

New Directions for Community Colleges • DOI: 10.1002/cc

A second example can be gleaned from a 1994 program begun by the NCAA, CHAMPS (Challenging Athletes' Minds for Personal Success). The program was designed to enhance the quality of the student athlete's academic experiences. These skills are transferable to all students in institutions of higher education. Five areas were identified as key components to address the needs of the student-athlete population: (1) academic excellence, (2) athletic excellence, (3) personal development, (4) career development, and (5) service.

Academic Advising. The role of the academic advisor is integral in the life of a student athlete. At the community college level, this role may be assumed by a student services advisor, a registrar, or even a coach. Athlete support programs or individuals fulfilling this role should serve to facilitate learning opportunities that take place in the classroom (Carodine, Almond, and Gratto, 2001; Reyes, 1997). Student athletes are often susceptible to the influence of teammates, mentors, and peers. This may be of special importance for students at the community college level because of the increased likelihood of being a first-generation college student or member of an underrepresented group (Kornspan and Etzel, 2001).

An essential role of the academic support staff is to examine and evaluate the academic progress of each student athlete. One effective method for this monitoring is use of a progress report system between student services staff and college faculty. These progress reports may be given to college faculty as often as two to four times each semester for staff members to gain valuable insight into the student athletes' academic progress. Progress reports allow academic advisors to evaluate students' progress and make provisions for tutoring, mentoring, or additional academic support measures as needed. This system of evaluation and progress monitoring at the community college level may be coordinated by a variety of personnel, but ultimately it is essential to maintain and monitor the academic success of these students.

One form of advising called "intrusive advising" (Glennen, 1976) has emerged as an effective form of academic support (Heisserer and Parette, 2002). Intrusive advising is premised on the academic advisor and the student sharing responsibility for student academic performance (Thomas and Minton, 2004; Hagedorn, in press). Intrusive advising includes a progress monitoring system where advisor and student continuously examine and evaluate academic progress throughout the semester and plan collaboratively. Student athletes, many of whom are academically underprepared when enrolling in college, may benefit greatly from the intrusive approach (Kramer and Upcraft, 1995). Ultimately, implementation of intrusive advising has been shown to improve the effectiveness of advising, enhance student academic skills, and increase retention (Earl, 1988; Hagedorn, in press).

Student-Athlete Counseling. One of the most fervent obstacles facing athletes is the ability to balance athletic and academic demands. The stresses imposed by athletic commitments may interfere with psychosocial and academic development. Of note is the fact that student athletes often report feelings of isolation, loneliness, and profound fear of failure both in the classroom and on the playing field (Simons, Rheenan, and Covington, 1999). The transition from high school to college may cause even those students with an exceptional academic record to struggle with the transition to college. The combination of the demands of the playing field, a traditionally underprepared academic background, and pressure from coaches, faculty, and passionate fans may result in a profound sense of despair and an increased likelihood of a student athlete becoming overwhelmed (Cantor and Prentice, 1996; Hewitt, 2002). To combat these issues, athletic departments and student support programs should engage student athletes in activities beyond the athletic field and their respective classes (Shurts and Shoffner 2004).

In many cases, the demanding schedule of the student athlete prevents participating in a range of general student activities because the majority of free time is spent in practice, group study sessions, weight training, and homework (Cantor and Prentice, 1996; Jordan and Denson, 1990). A recent conversation with one athlete revealed that her day began with class at 8:00 A.M. and did not allow a break, other than for meals, until 10:00 P.M., six days per week. One recommendation is to establish a system where student athletes report to existing personnel on campus (coaches, advisors, faculty) to assist with these issues.

Before developing and implementing strategies for student athlete counseling, it is advisable to conduct a comprehensive needs assessment of student athletes (Kornspan and Etzel, 2001). In addition, it is recommended that student services establish a collaborative partnership with clinical psychologists, mental health service providers, and special education professionals to introduce strategies for addressing the needs of student athletes with emotional and learning issues (Carodine, Almond, and Gratto, 2001).

Program Evaluation. Along with these recommendations, the student services support program should be evaluated annually. Effective evaluation strategies may include analyses of data pertaining to student retention, graduation, and professional and academic progress after leaving the institution ("Academic Support Programs . . . ," 1992). This process may be overseen by a board of trustees, directors, or even external evaluators, to ensure that the best interests of the students and the institution are being taken into account.

The Influence of the National Collegiate Athletic Association (NCAA)

In recent years, the NCAA has increased the minimum requirements for initial athletic eligibility and enrollment into four-year institutions for prospective college athletes (NCAA, 2008). The new NCAA rules, among them Proposition 16, require prospective students to have completed sixteen core courses while enrolled in high school—an increase from the previous requirement of fourteen core courses. Core courses are in the content areas of English, mathematics, natural and physical sciences, and social sciences. In addition to these course requirements, beginning in 2008 all recent high school graduates are required to have maintained a GPA of at least 2.0 in all sixteen core courses. Specific quantities of core courses must be completed with minimum grade requirements based on the student athlete's standardized college entrance exam scores. A sliding scale was developed to compensate for the limited variability of GPA and college entrance exam scores.

The NCAA, starting in August 2009, will require all member institutions to set minimum eligibility requirements for community college transfer students, including six credits of English and three credits of mathematics. This policy is currently implemented by member institutions of the Southeastern Athletic Conference (SEC), but it will become mandatory for all NCAA conferences in 2009. This change will make a universal policy for all community college transfers, which will eliminate some of the difficulty and confusion with student transfer to an institution in another athletic conference.

Prospective college athletes who do not meet these initial standards will be ineligible to participate as student athletes at a Division I institution. As an option, student athletes may select to enroll in a community college with hopes of ultimately transferring to a four-year school. If the option to attend a community college is selected and a student completes academic requirements leading to an associate degree, she or he will no longer be subjected to the initial NCAA athletic eligibility rules. Instead, the student must meet only the stipulations and requirements as outlined by the four-year institution for community college transfer students. Community college support services administrators must have knowledge of transfer policies and be familiar with these rules in order to best advise their student athletes. It is also imperative that community college student personal professionals keep abreast of the changing requirements initiated by NCAA and other athletic governing bodies that may hinder students' continued study and athletic participation at the four-year institution.

The NCAA and Community College Transfers. There are numerous reasons student athletes choose to start their postsecondary athletic career at the community college level. An institution's proximity to home, small collegial environment, athletic scholarship, encouragement from family and friends, professional athletic aspirations, limited athletic development or immaturity, academic preparedness, and the influence of a high school coach may all be factors in the decision-making process (Somers and others, 2006; Ryan, Groves, and Schneider, 2007). It is imperative that professionals at the community college be equipped to provide students with accurate academic advisement and have up-to-date knowledge of the various NCAA transfer rules and regulations.

NEW DIRECTIONS FOR COMMUNITY COLLEGES • DOI: 10.1002/cc

Additionally, because some student athletes begin a community college failing to meet minimum NCAA academic eligibility requirements, institutions should make a concerted effort to support and encourage students to improve their academic skills while attending the community college. This may include (but is not limited to) supporting students to successfully complete remediation or developmental course requirements.

Recommendations

The mission of an exemplary community college support services program for athletes should be to prepare students for life after college. To accomplish this mission, the program should provide and support quality programs and services that facilitate graduation or transfer to a four-year institution and promote overall development of student athletes. The focus of the support services is to further the personal, educational, and career development of student athletes.

To accomplish these goals, student athlete support services should include a number of components: academic advisement, academic mentoring, tutorial services, personal counseling and development, study skills, career exploration and development, and life management skills.

Academic Advisement. It is recommended that this include intrusive academic advising. Clear understanding of NCAA transfer rules is essential for advising community college athletes. This role may be assumed by current school personnel, among them student services advisors, faculty, coaches, and so on. This should not require additional personnel but may necessitate additional training of these personnel to equip them with the skills needed to meet the needs of student athletes.

Academic Mentoring. Collegiality and increased academic confidence may be achieved when peer academic support structures are implemented. Navigating the transition from secondary to postsecondary schooling generates challenges that go beyond mere academics, notably interactions with faculty, test preparation, and time management. The mentoring relationship may assist student athletes with time management, study skills, and overall organizational skills during their first collegiate semester. This role may be assumed by current school personnel (student services advisors, faculty, former student athletes, and coaches).

Tutorial Services. Group and individual tutorial services serve to augment the academic performance of student athletes, who are often confronted with scheduling conflicts that have an impact on attendance and participation in academic enrichment opportunities. Tutors are typically graduate students, upperclassmen, volunteers, and even school staff identified by professors or departments as having the necessary expertise in the specific discipline. Many schools are creating academic centers designed to lend academic support to student athletes. Such centers are designed with a holistic approach that assists the total academic and personal development of student athletes. At the community college level, it is recommended that academic advising resources and tutoring centers be made available to student athletes to ensure that they are making satisfactory progress toward their current degree and future endeavors.

Personal Counseling and Development. The life of a student athlete is frequently wrought with intense pressure, anxiety, and isolation from the general student population. Counseling services may greatly assist in nurturing the emotional well-being of the student athlete.

Study Skills. Quite often, it is not *what* students are studying but *how* they are studying that influences their academic success. Study skills development is essential to advancing the academic success of the student athlete. Exemplary programs not only assist students with content but also, and more importantly, demonstrate the most effective study and academic preparation skills.

Career Exploration and Development. Throughout the academic and athletic career of a student athlete, a strong emphasis must be placed on career planning and development. Exemplary student support programs help student athletes determine academic and personal goals in preparation for the culmination of their playing days.

Life Management Skills. Exemplary programs equip student athletes with the skills necessary to overcome obstacles and accept ownership of their own success. Many exemplary institutions have employed a life skills coordinator with the intention of offering valuable insight to student athletes about life after college. In a community college, it is recommended that the athletic department collaborate with the career services and life skill services offered on campus. These professionals conduct seminars and workshops designed to assist with issues ranging from graduate school preparation to financial management. Life skills coordinators may also guide students through the career exploration process.

Conclusion

On the basis of the increase in students attending community colleges and the growing desire of these students to transfer to a four-year institution, it seems essential that academic support units be examined to determine if they are equipped to meet needs. The CHAMPS Life Skills Program of Excellence sets benchmarks that all institutions should strive to meet. Addressing these areas will supply students with the necessary resources to be successful in transferring and in the professional world. Studies have clearly identified the importance of providing academic and personal enhancement services to students and student athletes alike (Keim and Strickland, 2004; Carodine, Almond, and Gratto, 2001). Research has further suggested that many community colleges make available more resources and focus on recruitment as opposed to retention (Fike and Fike, 2008). This is troubling because retention is vital for an institution's financial stability, sustaining academic programs, and ultimately the student graduation rate. As the educational landscape continues to change, so too should academic support units. Support programs must continuously assess programs and resources to ensure that they are meeting the diverse needs of the students who rely so heavily on their services and expertise for success both on and off the field or court of play (Harden and Pina-Tallmon, 1988).

References

"Academic Support Programs for Student Athletes." *Journal of Sport Management*, 1992, 6(1), 75.

Ashburn, E. "To Increase Enrollment Community Colleges Add More Sports." *Chronicle of Higher Education*, 2007, 44(53), A31.

Cantor, N., and Prentice, D. "The Life of the Modern-Day Student-Athlete: Opportunities Won and Lost." In Princeton Conference on Higher Education. Princeton, N.J.: Princeton University Press, 1996.

Carodine, K., Almond, K., and Gratto, K. "College Student Athlete Success Both in and out of the Classroom." In M. F. Howard-Hamilton and S. K. Watt (eds.), *Student Services for Athletes*. New Directions for Student Services, no. 93. San Francisco: Jossey-Bass, 2001.

Earl, W. R. "Intrusive advising of freshmen in academic difficulty." *NACADA Journal*, 1988, 8(2), 27–33.

Fike, D. S., and Fike, R. "Predictors of First-Year Student Retention in the Community College." *Community College Review*, 2008, 36, 68–88.

Gaston-Gayles, J. "Examining Academic and Athletic Motivation Among Student Athletes at a Division I University." *Journal of College Student Development*, 2004, 45(1), 75–83.

Glennen, R. E. "Intrusive College Counseling." *School Counselor*, 1976, 24, 48–50.

Gunn, E. L., and Eddy, J. P. "Student Services for Intercollegiate Athletics." *College Student Affairs Journal*, 1989, 9, 36–44.

Hagedorn, L.S. "The pursuit of student success: Community college interventions, supports and programs." In John C. Smart (ed.), *Higher Education: Handbook of Theory and Research*. New York: Agathon, in press.

Harden, H., and Pina-Tallmon, J. "A Comprehensive Academic Support Program for the Student-Athlete." *Journal of College Student Development*, 29 (March 1988): 173–174.

Heisserer, D.L., & Parette, P. "Advising At-Risk Students in College and University Settings." *College Student Journal*, 2002, 36, 69–83.

Hewitt, K. A. "Factors Associated with Academic Performance and Retention of Academically 'At-Risk' Freshman Student-Athletes." (Ph.D. diss., Washington State University, 2002).

Hobneck, C., Mudge, L., & Turchi, M. "Improving Student Athlete Academic Success and Retention." (Ph.D. diss., St. Xavier University, 2003).

Jenkins, R. "Athletics Aren't a Luxury at Community Colleges." *Chronicle of Higher Education*, Mar. 24, 2006, p. 13.

Jordan, J. M., and Denson, E. L. "Student Services for Athletes: A Model for Enhancing Student Athletes' Experiences." *Journal of Counseling and Development*, 1990, 69, 95–97.

Keim, M., and Strickland, J. "Support Services for Two-Year College Student-Athletes." *College Student Journal*, 2004, 38, 36–43.

Knapp, T., and Raney, J. "Student Athletes at Two-Year Colleges: Transcript Analysis of Grades and Credits." *Community College Journal of Research and Practice*, 1988, 12(2), 99–105.

Kornspan, A. S., and Etzel, E. F. "The Relationship of Demographic and Psychological Variables to Career Maturity of Junior College Student-Athletes." *Journal of College Student Development* 42, no. 2 (March-April 2001): 122–132.

Kramer, G. L., and Upcraft, M. L. *First-Year Student Academic Advising: Patterns in the Present, Pathways to the Future.* Columbia, S.C.: National Resource Center for the Freshman Year Experience and Students in Transition, 1995.

Lally, P., and Kerr, G. "Career Planning, Athletic Identity, and Student Role Identity of Intercollegiate Student Athletes." *Research Quarterly for Exercise & Sport*, 2005, 3, 278–285.

Lenz, J., and Shy, J. "Career Services and Athletics: Collaborating to Meet the Needs of Student-Athletes." *N.A.C.E Journal* 63, no. 3 (2003): 36–40.

Mumford, V. "Promoting Equity and Access in 2-Year College Intercollegiate Athletic Programs." *Community College Journal of Research and Practice*, 2006, 30, 213–222.

Reyes, N. "Holding on to What They've Got." *Black Issues in Higher Education*, 1997, 13(6), 36–40.

Ryan, C., Groves, D., and Schneider, R. "A Study of Factors That Influence High School Athletes to Choose a College or University, and a Model for the Development of Player Decisions." *College Student Journal*, 2007, 41(3), 95–109.

Shurts, W. M., and Shoffner, M. "Providing Career Counseling for Collegiate Student-Athletes: A Learning Theory Approach." *Journal of Career Development*, 2004, 31(2), 95–109.

Simons, H. D., Rheenen, D. V., and Covington, M. B. "Academic Motivation and the Student Athlete." *Journal of College Student Development*, 1999, 40(2), 151–161.

Somers, P., Haines, K. and Keene, B. "Towards a Theory of Choice for Community College Students." *Community College Journal of Research and Practice* 30, no. 1 (January 2006): 53–67.

Thomas, C., and Minton, J. "Intrusive Advisement: A Model for Success at John A. Logan College." *Office of Community College Research and Leadership*, 2004, 15(2), 1–16.

Umbach, P., Palmer, M., Kuh, G., and Hannah, S. "Intercollegiate Athletes and Effective Educational Practices: Winning Combination or Losing Effort." *Research in Higher Education*, 2006, 47(6), 709–733.

JASON STORCH *is the assistant director of academic services within the University Athletic Association at the University of Florida.*

MATTHEW OHLSON *is a doctoral candidate and director of C.A.M.P. Gator, the Collegiate Achievement Mentoring Program at the University of Florida.*

NEW DIRECTIONS FOR COMMUNITY COLLEGES • DOI: 10.1002/cc

8

This final chapter of this volume takes a critical and candid look at athletics at the community college and discusses the place of athletics during the most uncertain economic times since the 1930s.

Conclusions and Parting Words from the Editors

Linda Serra Hagedorn, David Horton, Jr.

This volume provides information and perspective on community college athletics, a topic that has been sorely ignored by the literature. As you progressed through the volume you may have noted what appears to be a positive bias to the volume. In other words, there is a conspicuous imbalance in the discussion of the positives and negatives of having athletics at a two-year campus. In this last chapter, and as parting words, we take a highly critical look at athletics and respond to the question of whether contemporary community colleges should continue to maintain athletic programs, especially in times of financial constraint. For balance, we have chosen to focus on the negatives. We feel it is important to present a balanced picture in support of the more than seventy thousand community college athletes.

Confronting the Evil Twin of Community College Athletic Programs

Athletics and colleges have been so intrinsically intertwined that it is often hard to think of one without the other. Indeed, the first mention of sport as related to college was an 1843 record of a boat club at Yale University (Lewis, 1970). The historical records also include accounts of athletics among the earliest community colleges. For example, the National Junior College Athletic Association (NJCAA) was established in 1939 with a track and field meet (Reapple, Peery, and Hohman, 1982). Today, almost half of all community colleges offer some form of intercollegiate athletics (Community

New Directions for Community Colleges, no. 147, Fall 2009 © 2009 Wiley Periodicals, Inc.
Published online in Wiley InterScience (www.interscience.wiley.com) • DOI: 10.1002/cc.380

College Review, n.d.). Understandably, the long history replete with inter-linking makes the very thought of divorcing sport and college hinge on the heretical. However, in this section we analyze the situation sans fanfare or devotee emotions.

Money, Money, Money

At the time of this writing, the United States is engulfed in the worst recession since the Great Depression of the 1930s ("The Global Slumpometer," 2008). Budget cuts for higher education in general and community colleges in particular abound in almost every state. College administrators are examining programs under high magnification to find ways to either cut expenses or eliminate them. Athletic programs that are not revenue producers may therefore be destined for the chopping block.

It is a fact that large university athletic programs depend on private donations (Wolverton, 2009), a practice that is very rare among community college athletics. In this time of economic woe, it is not a coincidence that at least eight major university athletic programs are currently conducting capital campaigns to raise more than $100 million to continue to support sports programs (Wolverton, 2009). Adding to the problem, community colleges are less likely than their four-year counterparts to participate in sports that produce revenue. As Horton points out in his chapter in this volume, only 4 percent of community colleges with athletic programs report annual earned revenues above $150,000. And of course, even the most profitable community college athletic program produces but a fraction of the revenue enjoyed by universities in the Big Ten and Big Twelve athletic conferences. As such, most of the community college programs are not self-sustaining and require external funds for their operation. In times of financial constraint, the avenues for finding resources are few and narrow. Hence community college athletic programs may be seen as less integral to the mission of the community college and, in the most negative of lights, may even be viewed as a financial drag.

The Typical Community College Student

Community colleges were not designed to serve the traditional student. We define *traditional* as right out of high school, attending full-time, and without outside employment or significant family responsibilities. Quite the contrary: community colleges serve a range of students, with the majority being part-time, employed, and those entrusted with the financial support of others. The typical community college student leads a life that is not centered on the college campus but rather includes college as an aspect of life, though not its essence.

The nature and intensity of sport participation precludes from participation the majority of adult learners, e-learners, working students, older students, and those with intense family constraints. Because NJCAA eligibility requires full-time enrollment status, the majority of community college students would be ruled ineligible. Thus athletic programs may not serve the pool of students who are more likely to attend community colleges. It may also be worthy of note that current NCAA rules preclude use of online courses to meet Division I eligibility requirements to play after transfer to the four-year institution (NCAA, 2008). Further, in order to play directly after transfer to a Division I university, students must have been enrolled in at least twelve units per semester in transfer-level courses; thus part-time transfer hopefuls and those in developmental coursework cannot be fully integrated into their teams on transfer. In times of financial constraint, administrators may need to consider their mission, their majority student pool, and thus the audience that benefits from supported programs.

The Practical Arts and Workforce Curricula

Although many students attend a community college as a stepping stone to a four-year university, a large number are enrolled in terminal programs that teach vocational arts and job skills. The workforce development programs of colleges provide the appropriate training for industry sectors within their service area (Government Accountability Office, 2008). Workforce programs are often short-term and intense and frequently conducted at the industrial site. Programs may begin and end at any time of the year because they are often not tied to the traditional semester structure. Students enrolled in these programs are likely not able to participate in athletics, are ineligible on the basis of NJCAA rules, and probably have less desire to play sports. As the economy worsens community colleges are likely to expand workforce development programs and hence increase the proportion of students with workforce goals and enrollment patterns that are not NJCAA-eligible.

Community Goodwill

A credible argument in favor of community college athletics is their provision of community goodwill. Of course, we agree heartily with the connection, but through our critical spectacles we see that athletic programs do not stand alone in the provision of community resources. Community goodwill is also doled out through links to jobs and training, work with homeless shelters and faith-based organizations, and at some colleges for work in prisons. Supported through public taxes, the nonacademic endeavors of community colleges will continue to come under heavier scrutiny as dollars become scarcer. It is true that some community colleges use sporting events as a means of community fellowship, but in times when unemployment is rising faster than pundits anticipated (Rugaber, 2008) it is unlikely that the unemployed community citizen is awaiting the next local college sporting event.

Ubiquitous Academic Developmental Problems

Within some community college districts, close to 80 percent of students are enrolled in at least one developmental-level course (Adelman, 2004; Breneman and Costrell, 1998; Schmidt, 2006). Moreover, analyses of national data indicate that only 17 percent of high school seniors are proficient in mathematics and about twice that number (36 percent) achieve proficiency in reading (Braswell and others, 2001). Many researchers, policymakers, and college administrators admit that developmental education is one of the most complex and obstinate problems confronting contemporary community colleges (Kozeracki, 2002).

It is undeniable that community colleges have become the contemporary targets and relegated brokers of developmental education. The states of Arizona, California, Colorado, Florida, Georgia, Indiana, Kansas, Louisiana, New Mexico, New York, Massachusetts, South Carolina, Utah, and Virginia have instituted policies to either prevent or restrict remediation in the public university systems (Jenkins and Bowell, 2002). Other states are drafting similar policies.

Certainly the presence of a large number of students enrolled in "less than college level" instruction does not, and probably should not, preclude a thriving athletic program, but it does call into question whether students requiring deep academic support should be encouraged or allowed to participate in an extracurricular activity that will likely restrict study time and may force them to miss classes for games. Although it is true that community college athletic eligibility rules require students to maintain an adequate GPA in order to participate, there is no requirement in the level or type of courses in which students must maintain enrollment to play at the community college.

An important issue is that NCAA rules require not only that students transferring to Division I and II earn an average of twelve credits per enrolled semester while at the community college, but also that those credits *must* be transferable to the bachelor's degree. In other words, credits from courses classified as developmental or remedial will not count toward eligibility to play at Division I and II campuses. Thus many transfer students may be able to practice and receive athletically related aid post transfer but will be required to sit out a year of residence prior to full participation at the transfer location.

The problems of keeping college athletes academically eligible, as well as anecdotal stories of students who claim abuse, are fairly widespread. In response, a recent development in Division I is discussion of an academic progress rate for coaches (Sander, 2009). The NCAA has indicated that such a measure may be appropriate for reasons of public accountability. For university coaches, one of the measures the NCAA is considering is graduation rate among the athletes under the coach's supervision. If this policy should extend to the community college, it may be appropriate to use the measure of community college athletes' progression through developmental education.

Recruitment

Universities use athletic scholarships to entice athletes to enroll. Many athletic scholarships are the result of endowment income. As stated earlier, few community colleges can boast such endowed funds. Only community colleges within the NJCAA's Division I and II are able to award athletic aid. Division I colleges may offer up to a full "free ride" (that is, tuition, fees, books, room and board, and transportation) while colleges in Division II are limited to college-related expenses (tuition, fees, books). As seen in Table 2 of the first chapter in this volume, by Bush and colleagues, even though the majority of athletic programs may offer aid, 37 percent of community colleges participating in intercollegiate athletics cannot offer athletic scholarships.

High-profile athletic programs are often touted as an effective attraction that acts as an enhancer to recruiting students (Toma and Cross, 1998). Termed the "front door" of the university, specifically men's basketball and football are arguably the most visible and renowned areas of the university. High-profile spectator sports are responsible for name recognition and attracting tuition dollars—often from out-of-state students whose only exposure to the college is through sports coverage. It may be true, especially in rural areas, that community college athletics attract some students to enroll, but the low coverage of these programs outside their service area is not likely to attract additional students.

Community college athletic programs may recruit students with the expectation of subsequent transfer to a large university with Division I sports. According to statistics reported by the NCAA, in 2006–07 more than six thousand students transferred from community colleges to colleges or universities and their Division I sports programs (Wieberg, 2008). Unfortunately, the NCAA also reports that transfer students are significantly more likely to become academically ineligible. In fact, more than 11 percent of transfers in men's basketball and football became academically ineligible to play during academic year 2006–07 (Wieberg, 2008). So even though athletics may be a recruiting tool for some students, it should be noted that transfer is a difficult path for any student, and when an athletic schedule is superimposed it may be the breaking point for students with a shaky academic record.

Since 1965, the NCAA has instituted a number of policies aimed at increasing the quality of students who are recruited and who subsequently participate in athletic programs at the various levels (Heck and Takahashi, 2006). These minimum standards, intended to increase students' degree completion, often exceed the minimum requirements of the institution's admissions office (DeBrock, Hendricks, and Koenker, 1996; Heck and Takahashi, 2006). However, such safeguards are not currently in place for student participation at the community college. Minimum academic requirements serve as a preliminary screening process to protect both the student and the institution from future failure; only students who are qualified to handle their academic studies and athletic participation are considered. Unlike four-year institutional governing bodies, boards that govern athletics at the community college have neglected to see the importance of these preliminary measures. If providing increased access to higher education is the goal of athletic programs, so should be consideration of a mechanism to ensure students transfer to, and are prepared for academic studies at, four-year institutions.

The Faucet Phenomenon

Community college students are much more likely than their four-year counterparts to abandon their studies for a semester, a year, or even longer and then return to their program. For some students this on-again, off-again behavior can only be likened to a faucet. Such enrollment practices do not coordinate well with an athletic program. In fact, as indicated earlier, if a student has not earned an average of twelve semester credits for each term enrolled at the community college, he or she must complete a year of residence at the transfer location prior to full athletic participation (NCAA, 2008).

NJCAA rules were clearly established with a more traditional student in mind. Swirling patterns of transfer, faucet-type enrollment, part-time semesters, and other behaviors not uncommon among community college students do not mix well with athletic requirements.

Institutional Priorities

During the current economic crunch, community college administrators and others are rewriting strategic plans and planning principles, and determining institutional priorities. Athletics departments of major universities aware of the shifting environment of financial stability are rampaging to increase their sports endowment account not only to compensate for the recent market downturn that has devastated all endowments but also to plan for necessary capital expenses (Wolverton, 2009). Prominent universities acknowledge that sports are a major part of their offerings, but community colleges may have to take a second look at how they can maintain athletics amidst a sea of other priorities.

USA Group Noel-Levitz performs an annual National Institutional Priorities Study to determine the areas that faculty, administrators, and staff perceive as the most important institutional priorities. Consistently their survey of community, junior, and technical colleges found that participants rated (1) concern for the individual and (2) instructional effectiveness as the top items for their college's priorities (USA Group Noel-Levitz, 1999, 2003). Athletic programs may need to establish how they fit into these important institutional aspects.

In this era of economic concern and retrenchment, community colleges must revisit their unit priorities and clearly state how they mesh with those of the institution. Where the priorities of the unit do not precisely meet those at the institutional level, it may be necessary for funding to be left to the unit. Hence community college athletics may have to seek funding for their very existence. To be included in the institutional priorities, athletics must argue that they are integral to academic quality and student success.

Conclusions: The Warning

This is a warning call. This concluding chapter has presented the most negative of scenes and may be accused of creating an atmosphere of gloom and doom, but we present these words with a purpose: to indicate the enormous challenges confronting the very existence of community college athletic programs and to spur quick and absolute action. We do not condone the abandonment of community college athletics; else we would never have edited this volume. Rather, out of concern for these programs we want to present the obstacles and the chance of their demise if swift action is not taken. We promote athletic departments embarking on a series of self-examinations beginning with a SWOT analysis (strengths, weaknesses, external opportunities, and threats) that acknowledges how the unit aligns with institutional priorities emphasizing the effect on all campus constituents, including students, faculty, administrators, and even trustees. Second, we promote community college athletic units thoughtfully determining their strategic goals and carefully documenting successes and cases of nonsuccess. Finally, community college athletic programs must determine the strategic directions they will take in the short and long run, with a watchful eye on financial exigency.

For closing words we wish to borrow from the wisdom of two famous men from the world of sports and athletics. Knute Rockne, the Notre Dame football player and coach, admonished us to "build up your weaknesses until they become your strong points." Finally, these words of baseball great Yogi Berra can be an inspiration: "It ain't over till it's over!"

References

Adelman, C. *Principal Indicators of Student Academic Histories in Postsecondary Education, 1972–2000.* Washington, D.C.: Institute of Education Sciences, U.S. Department of Education, 2004.

Braswell, J. S., Lutkus, A. D., Grigg, W. S., Santapau, S. L., Tay-Lim, B., and Johnson, M. *The Nation's Report Card: Mathematics 2000* (NCES 2001–517). Washington, D.C.: National Center for Education Statistics, U.S. Department of Education, 2001.

Breneman, D., and Costrell, R. *Remediation in Higher Education.* Washington, D.C.: Thomas B. Fordham, 1998.

Community College Review. (n.d.). "Athletics in Community Colleges." Retrieved Nov. 24, 2008, from http://www.communitycollegereview.com/articles/10.

DeBrock, L., Hendricks, W., and Koenker, R. "The Economics of Persistence: Graduation Rates of Athletes as Labor Market Choice." *Journal of Human Resources,* 1996, *31,* 513–539.

"The Global Slumpometer." *Economist,* Nov. 6, 2008. Retrieved Nov. 24, 2008, from http://www.economist.com/finance/economicsfocus/displaystory.cfm?story_id=12553076.

Government Accountability Office. "Workforce Development." 2008. Retrieved Nov. 24, 2008, from http://www.gao.gov/new.items/d08547.pdf.

Heck, R. H., and Takahashi, R. "Examining the Impact of Proposition 48 on Graduation Rates in Division 1a Football and Program Recruiting Behavior: Testing a Policy Change Model." *Educational Policy*, 2006, 20(4), 587–614.

Jenkins, D., and Boswell, K. *State Policies on Community College Remedial Education: Findings from a National Survey*. Denver: Center for Community College Policy, Education Commission of the States, 2002.

Kozeracki, C. "ERIC Review: Issues in Developmental Education." *Community College Review*. Retrieved Jan. 29, 2009, http://findarticles.com/p/articles/mi_m0HCZ/is_4_29/ai_86743295.

Lewis, G. "The Beginning of Organized Collegiate Sport." *American Quarterly*, 1970, 22(2), 222–229.

NCAA. *Transfer 101*. Indianapolis: National Collegiate Athletic Association, 2008.

Reapple, R., Peery, D., and Hohman, H. "Athletics in Community and Junior Colleges." In J. Frey (ed.), *The Governance of Intercollegiate Athletics*. West Point, N.Y.: Leisure Press, 1982.

Rugaber, C. S. "Unemployment Claims Rising Faster Than Expected as Recession Deepens." *Huffington Post*, Oct. 23, 2008. Retrieved Nov. 25, 2008, from http://www.huffingtonpost.com/2008/10/23/unemployment-claims-risin_n_137336.html.

Sander, L. "NCAA to Develop Another 'Academic-Progress Rate'—for Coaches." *Chronicle of Higher Education,* Jan. 19, 2009, n.p.

Schmidt, P. "Powerful Forces Draw Academe into the Fray." *Chronicle of Higher Education,* Mar. 10, 2006, p. B4.

Toma, J. D., and Cross, M. E. "Intercollegiate Athletics and Student College Choice: Exploring the Impact of Championship Seasons on Undergraduate Applications." *Research in Higher Education,* 1998, 39(6), 633–661.

Wieberg, S. "Transfers' Academics on Radar for NCAA." *USA Today*, Nov. 12, 2008, p. A6.

Wolverton, B. "For Athletics, a Billion-Dollar Goal Line." *Chronicle of Higher Education,* Jan. 23, 2009, p. B1.

USA Group Noel-Levitz. "National Institutional Priorities Report." 1999. Retrieved November 30, 2008, from https://www.noellevitz.com/NR/rdonlyres/CC985E48–96A0–4DB3–954D-052B1188803B/0/IPS_99_report.pdf.

USA Group Noel-Levitz. "National Institutional Priorities Report." 2003. ERIC Reproduction Services ED479159.

LINDA SERRA HAGEDORN *is professor and director of the Research Institute for Studies in Education (RISE) at Iowa State University.*

DAVID HORTON, JR., *is an assistant professor in the Department of Counseling and Higher Education at Ohio University.*

INDEX

Why Wait to Make Great Discoveries

When you can make them in an instant with
Wiley InterScience® Pay-Per-View and ArticleSelect™

Now you can have instant, full-text access to an extensive collection of journal articles or book chapters available on Wiley InterScience. With Pay-Per-View and ArticleSelect™, there's no limit to what you can discover...

ArticleSelect™ is a token-based service, providing access to full-text content from non-subscribed journals to existing institutional customers (EAL and BAL)

Pay-per-view is available to any user, regardless of whether they hold a subscription with Wiley InterScience.

Benefits:

• Access online full-text content from journals and books that are outside your current library holdings
• Use it at home, on the road, from anywhere at any time
• Build an archive of articles and chapters targeted for your unique research needs
• Take advantage of our free profiled alerting service the perfect companion to help you find specific articles in your field as soon as they're published
• Get what you need instantly no waiting for document delivery
• Fast, easy, and secure online credit card processing for pay-per-view downloads
• Special, cost-savings for EAL customers: whenever a customer spends tokens on a title equaling 115% of its subscription price, the customer is auto-subscribed for the year
• Access is instant and available for 24 hours

WILEY
InterScience®
DISCOVER SOMETHING GREAT

www.interscience.wiley.com